# WINGS
# OF
# VALOR

## Real-Life Aviation Adventures in War and Peace

## Allan T. Duffin

published by

**duffin**|creative

los angeles

Published in the USA by
Duffin Creative
11684 Ventura Blvd #205
Studio City, CA 91604
Visit us on the Web at duffincreative.com

ISBN-10: 0692719407
ISBN-13: 978-0692719404

Printed in the United States of America

# TABLE OF CONTENTS

# OPERATIONS
# IN WARTIME
# AND PEACETIME

# AIR TO GROUND:
# TRANSPORTING PLANES

CHUCK MOSELY, ALSO KNOWN AS "CHUCKMO," tows things, but he isn't a tower in the traditional sense. He doesn't tow cars, trucks, vans or station wagons. He tows airplanes. Mosely's company, All Coast Aircraft Recovery, Inc., is based in Weirsdale, Fla.

Mosely works with three types of clients: insurance companies that need damaged aircraft transported to repair facilities, private owners who want their property moved from point to point, and museums that need to relocate historic aircraft.

### From Naval aviation to aircraft recovery

It's no surprise that Mosely works in an aviation-related field. His father flew Grumman F6F Hellcats during World War II. When he was old enough,

Mosely enlisted in the U.S. Navy, launching a military career that lasted 35 years.

"I started out as an aviation structural mechanic for my first 14 years," Mosely recalled. "I also flew as an aircrewman on SP-5B Martin Marlin sea patrol planes and DP-2E Lockheed Neptune target launch aircraft."

During the Vietnam War, Mosely was assigned to VF-114, a squadron that flew the F-4 Phantom fighter, aboard the aircraft carrier U.S.S. *Kitty Hawk*. Five years later he earned an officer's commission and supervised maintenance for various aircraft until his retirement from the Navy in 1998.

While he was an aircraft maintenance officer, Mosely worked closely with the Navy Museum in Pensacola, Fla. The museum temporarily loaned its retired military aircraft to other museums around the country.

After he retired, Mosely wanted to continue helping museums find and relocate airplanes for static display. He founded All Coast Aircraft Recovery to do just that. Along the way he expanded his company's offerings into private-property and insurance work.

### Equipment for the job

Often an aircraft needs to be taken apart before it can be loaded and driven to its destination. All Coast accomplishes most of its aircraft hauling by placing the components on pickup trucks. The company also has a special trailer, loaded with unique tools and equipment required to disassemble larger aircraft.

The size of the aircraft is a determining factor when planning a transport operation. "Large aircraft require large trucks, even when they are disassembled," Mosely continued. "In most cases we need multiple trucks to relocate a single aircraft."

Heavy hauling capability for All Coast is provided by two vendors: Les Chapman Transport, Inc., out of Blossom, Texas, and Skipper Shippers, Inc., out of Jenson Beach, Fla. "We have a very close and mutually supportive working relationship with both of these companies," explained Mosely. "These two companies also arrange and manage all of the permit and escort requirements."

What if the job requires a crane? Mosely again contracts with local providers. "Our crane requirements vary depending on the size and weight of the aircraft and any disassembled aircraft components," he explained.

All Coast also has a standard contract with United Rentals for jobs that require forklifts or man-lifts. United Rentals delivers and picks up the rental equipment at the job site.

**Human resources**

Depending on the type and size of the aircraft, Mosely gathers between 3 and 10 personnel for a recovery job. "I have a group of men who have worked with me since the formation of the company," said Mosely.

Mosely's staff isn't just familiar with how to load and tow an aircraft — each man is well qualified on the operation of the aircraft as well. All of Mosely's team members are aviation maintenance specialists who hold an FAA A&P (airframe and powerplant) license. Most of the team members hold private pilots' licenses, and half of them are FAA-certified to perform certain inspections on the aircraft.

"All of my team members have a lot of experience staging, loading, securing, and unloading the various aircraft for surface transportation," said Mosely. "A lot of [that experience] is gained through moving the same type of aircraft on multiple occasions."

During a recovery job, Mosely also assigns each of his staffers a collateral duty such as safety, HAZMAT, and rigging supervisor.

All Coast has been performing aircraft recovery and transport for 15 years, and Mosely isn't stopping anytime soon. "I and all of my team members thoroughly enjoy our line of work, as well as the people we meet and work with," he said.

**Facts and Figures**

• To lift the aircraft components, Mosely and his team use nylon harnesses of various lengths and strength ratings. "The harnesses are usually used in pairs," explained Mosely, "and are used as part of the individual rigging solutions along with the appropriate steel shackles and couplings." Mosely also uses steel cables when using a spreader bar for major lifts.

• "Major lifts" usually involve the aircraft fuselage, which usually requires a crane that's subcontracted from a local company. The cranes are normally in the 20,000 to 80,000 pound range depending on the type of aircraft being relocated.

• Lightest aircraft relocated: 1,500 pounds.

• Heaviest aircraft relocated: 75,800 pounds (empty). This was the C-130 Hercules cargo transport. "Of course, the various components after disassembly weigh less," said Mosely, "but the fuselage is still over 30,000 pounds!"

**Insurance Recovery**

Chuck Mosely's company, All Coast Aircraft Recovery, hauls busted aircraft for insurance companies, but fortunately these particular gigs aren't usually too complicated. "All of our aircraft relocation projects are planned well in advance," he explained, "and do not usually involve aircraft that have suffered extensive damage."

In June 2008, Mosely and his staff received a call from an insurance company, with a simple request: "Please relocate a privately-owned Cessna Citation Mustang (a small business aircraft that carries four to five passengers) from an airport in northern San Diego county."

The accident? While the aircraft was landing, it jumped the runway and came back down at an awkward angle. The main landing gear, flaps, and main wing assembly were damaged. "The mishap damage was of such extent," recalled Mosely, "that it rendered the aircraft as non-flyable until the damage was repaired."

The insurance company needed All Coast to disassemble, load, and transport the crippled aircraft to the Cessna Repair and Service Center in Sacramento, California — a distance of approximately 500 miles.

"My company pre-fabricated a fuselage transportation fixture — a cradle for the airplane to rest in — from drawings provided by Cessna," said Mosely. "This became a joint operation. Our team worked closely with representatives from the Cessna Repair and Service Center in order to transport the aircraft in a safe and protected manner." Mosely needed to make sure that no additional damage occurred to the airplane during transport.

After Mosely and his staff removed the wing assembly, they wrapped a harness around the fuselage and moved it gently onto the cradle, which had been mounted on a trailer. The wing assembly was lifted onto its own trailer, and both trucks then departed for Sacramento, where the procedure was reversed and the aircraft sections were unloaded so that Cessna could repair them.

"This is very typical of these type of aircraft relocation projects," said Mosely. "The joint team efforts are always very enjoyable operations. The other people whom we meet during our various adventures make our work unique and enjoyable."

## Moving a World War II Bomber

Mosely's favorite type of relocation project is the transport of historic aircraft for museums around the country. It's important, he said, "to preserve our nation's rich aviation heritage."

One of his company's projects involved the transport of a World War II B-17 four-engine bomber from the Smithsonian Institution in Washington, D.C., to the Mighty 8th Air Force Museum in Pooler, Ga.

"What was so unique about this aircraft relocation," Mosely recalled, "was the requirement to place the aircraft into the museum building a piece at a time, in the proper sequence to facilitate the reassembly in a restricted space."

Sounds simple enough. However, Mosely and his team had to roll the sections of the B-17 through a tunnel that was just 10 feet high and 14 feet wide, then reassemble the aircraft inside the museum.

On another occasion Mosely and his team transported and reassembled a B-25 medium bomber and a B-17 inside the newly constructed display building at the National WWII Museum in New Orleans, La. After that, Crownpoint, Inc., of Sun Valley, Calif., hoisted the two aircraft on wires so that the B-25 and B-17 hung from the ceiling.

"What made this task unique," said Mosely, "was that we had to move both aircraft into the building through another small opening, one piece at a time. After that we reassembled both aircraft and Crownpoint hoisted them 35 feet into the air, into their display positions."

The component parts of the B-25 and B-17 were delivered to the museum on flatbed trailers — regular rollback trucks such as those used for vehicle recovery — and also by forklift. All of the individual components were on mobile dolly fixtures so they could be relocated on the display floor after they were unloaded.

Another challenge during this relocation job: The building was still under construction, and Mosely's team had to work around 300 other people. "There were workers and craftsmen of various professions all around us — drywall installers, air conditioning technicians, electricians!"

# LANDING
# IN BAGHDAD

IMAGINE YOURSELF AS A PASSENGER IN AN AIRCRAFT on final approach into one of the most dangerous airports in the world. Looking out the window you see the flaps extend and feel the landing gear drop down and lock into place. Your aircraft rolls abruptly to one side and begins spinning downward like a power drill. You brace for impact, but suddenly the wheels hit with the ground and the airplane rolls to a stop on the runway. Why the dramatic landing? You've just avoided being shot down by a surface-to-air missile. Welcome to Baghdad International Airport.

Hundreds of civilian aircraft launch and land at Baghdad International every week. Outside the heavily defended airfield perimeter are bands of insurgents who target civilian and military aircraft with surface-to-air missiles. To avoid being knocked out of the sky, pilots utilize an old, trusted tactic: the spiral, or corkscrew, landing approach. Once the plane arrives at an altitude just out of missile range, the pilot banks sharply and descends toward the runway in a slow, tight circle. During the spiral the crew keeps an eye out for other air traffic — and for anything coming at them from the ground. The pilot executes several midair rotations, one after the other. Timing his approach carefully, he pulls out of the final rotation, straightens out, and touches down on the runway.

Though it sounds like a maneuver for the barnstorming acrobat in a flying circus, the corkscrew is actually a straightforward tactic that uses the pilot's existing toolbox of skills. With a little on-the-job training, spiraling down to the runway becomes second nature. "We time the rate of descent to keep the maneuver as short as possible and not overfly the limits of the airport," says Kurt Neuenschwander, international chief pilot for Air Serv International, a humanitarian nonprofit organization that transports relief workers and supplies into Baghdad. "We slow down and configure the aircraft for maximum stability, and stay within the normal parameters of the aircraft – normal bank angle, airspeed and rate of descent."

Initially the spiral was used only sporadically by pilots flying into Baghdad International Airport — until a near-disaster convinced everyone to give it a second look. In November 2003, a shoulder-fired surface-to-air missile ignited a fuel tank on an Airbus A300 cargo jet that had just left the runway. The resulting fireball set the left wing ablaze and knocked out all hydraulic systems. With thick funnels of smoke pouring from their airplane, the crew was able to come about and make an emergency landing — just barely.

Following the Airbus incident —the first civilian aircraft in postwar Iraq forced down due to a missile strike — most of the pilots flying into Baghdad quickly adopted the corkscrew as a standard evasive maneuver. The tactic is nothing new, dating back at least to the Vietnam War. "The spiral has been used for years into airports that have been secured militarily," says Paul Botha, chief pilot for AirQuarius, a South African firm that operates twin-engine Fokker F28s for Royal Jordanian Airlines. "I first became aware of it during the war between South Africa and the South West Africa People's Organization (SWAPO) in Namibia during the 1980s. Whenever we took off or landed we would execute multiple tight turns in order to decrease the possibility of being shot down." Kurt Neuenschwander of Air Serv began using the unique approach pattern to avoid small arms fire during the Sudanese civil war in 1994. "We were flying relief operations in and out of the country. In many villages where we landed, rebel forces were within a mile away and knew that we were coming."

Viewed from the ground, an aircraft on spiral approach appears to be making a measured, continuous turn. But for passengers inside the aircraft, the corkscrew can be intimidating. "You have no forward-looking vision," notes Neuenschwander. "So if you're looking out the side windows you're seeing either the sky or the ground. A lot of people tense up, especially if they don't have much flying experience." Journalist Betsy Hiel flew into Baghdad on an Air Serv aircraft and remembered "a woman across the aisle gritting her teeth so hard that she snapped one tooth off!"

On the other hand, the maneuver isn't a white-knuckle ride for everyone. "A very observant passenger might notice the prolonged maintenance of the bank, but nothing more," says Paul Botha. For frequent flyers, the spiral descent can become an exciting experience. "Coming in on a corkscrew affords a great view of Baghdad and of the airport," notes Thanassis Cambanis, who has flown in and out of Baghdad more than a dozen times while covering Iraq for the *Boston Globe*. "To me, the plane doesn't feel like it's descending any faster than usual, so it's not too frightening."

So if you fly into Baghdad International Airport in the near future, be prepared to experience some aerial acrobatics — and keep an eye out the window for missiles rushing at you from the ground. "You don't want to be a victim of circumstance," explains Kurt Neuenschwander. "Spiraling in can save your life."

# PAPER BULLETS:
# AERIAL LEAFLET DROPS
# IN AFGHANISTAN AND IRAQ

On December 3, 2007, a U.S. Air Force C-130 rumbled over the Iraqi landscape. Inside the airplane, two crewmembers braced themselves in front of the open troop door. When they were over the drop zone, they shoved a heavy cardboard box out of the airplane. The box broke apart in midair, and thousands of slips of paper scattered across the sky, floating down into the villages below.

The leaflets were tiny wanted posters, warning Iraqis on the ground that U.S. and coalition forces were hunting for three specific insurgents—wanted for planting improvised explosive devices (IEDs) and executing sniper attacks—and that citizens should not protect them. In one day, the C-130 crew deployed over one million leaflets across 10 drop zones in Iraq.

The results were immediate. "Within hours of the drop," U.S. Air Force Lieutenant Colonel Elizabeth Kavanagh, an information operations planner, told the American Forces Press Service, "reports were received of individuals arriving at Iraqi police stations with leaflets in hand." Kavanagh added that Iraqi citizens were phoning a tip line with information about suspected militia members and the locations of IEDs.

During the previous May, a C-130 aircrew wore night-vision goggles as they pitched 80,000 leaflets into the dark skies over the Helmand province in southwestern Afghanistan. "There is no honor in fighting alongside the enemies of Afghanistan," read the 6-by-4 inch (15 x 10 cm) flyers, which were directed at Taliban insurgents in the region. The flip side of the leaflet read, "The ANSF (Afghan National Security Forces) and ISAF (International Security Assistance Force) are ridding Helmand of the foreign Taliban."

Over Iraq and Afghanistan, coalition ground and air units create and drop leaflets to disseminate information, collect data about troop movements, and puncture the enemy's will to fight. The Iraq drop in December was requested by a Polish psychological operations unit, while U.S. Army personnel asked for the leaflet mission over Afghanistan. During the Helmand drop, leaflets were scattered over a 0.62-mile (1 km) radius. The leaflets are typically launched over rural or hard-to-reach regions, where colorful pictures mixed with text convey the message regardless of whether the recipient can read. "There is some evidence that the best way to reach large numbers of people who may or may not be literate is through aerial leaflets," says Sergeant Major Herbert Friedman, a 26-year U.S. Army veteran and psychological operations expert.

**Targeting with "paper bullets"**

Getting the leaflets to fall in a certain area is part art and part science. Planners take into account the size, shape and falling speed of the leaflet as well as environmental conditions like wind speed and direction. "I had a friend who dropped leaflets on North Korea who believed that he could place 100,000 leaflets on Kim Jong Il's doorstep at exactly 0700 if he had to," says Friedman. "He was exaggerating, but perhaps not by much."

The target varies with the purpose of the leaflets. "If you have enemy on a mountain top," explains Friedman, "that's where you need to drop your leaflets. On the other hand, if you want to convince civilians, as the U.S. did in Haiti in 1994, then you drop them directly over Port-au-Prince." One of the leaflets prepared for that mission featured a black-and-white photograph of exiled President Jean-Bertrand Aristide. "The warmth of reconciliation with the return of President Aristide," read part of the text on the opposite side—a missive, written in the Creole language, directed toward the civilian population.

During Operations Desert Shield and Storm in 1990–1991, "there were thousands of Iraqis that surrendered with leaflets in their hands," notes Friedman. "They surrendered to passing helicopters, news people or anyone else they could find." Well aware of the effectiveness of the coalition leaflet program, during Operation Iraqi Freedom the Iraqi government threatened to imprison or kill anyone who kept any of the leaflets that coalition aircraft rained down on the countryside.

Enforcement of the Iraq no-fly zones in the years leading up to Operations Iraq Freedom and Enduring Freedom included leaflet drops that urged Iraqi military personnel not to interfere with coalition aircraft or target them with radar. On March 10, 2003—eight days before coalition forces would invade the country —aircraft dropped 240,000 leaflets near Tall Afar and Saddam Lake, areas heavy with anti-aircraft activity. "Iraqi air defense positions which fire on coalition aircraft or activate air defense radar will be attacked and destroyed," read the leaflets.

With ongoing military operations in Afghanistan, leaflet drops were a recurring event. In July 2007, NATO aircraft dropped leaflets over Musa Qala, a village that had been held by the Taliban for nearly a year. The leaflets warned residents of impending attacks by coalition forces and encouraged them to evacuate. By December, following a final leaflet drop and a weeklong battle, British, American and Afghan forces captured the town as Taliban troops withdrew.

## Designing a leaflet

The design of a leaflet involves psychological as well as pragmatic considerations. "The simplest things, such as a picture and basic information, get the meaning across very quickly and increase the probability of contacting a large portion of the populace in the targeted area at one time," Kavanagh said after the December 2007 leaflet drop over Iraq. Recent leaflet designs have included photographs of individuals and families, cartoon drawings and composite artwork depicting cause-and-effect scenarios. Printed on small slices of paper, the messages are created to catch the eye after the leaflets have fluttered to the ground.

According to Friedman, basic design elements are incorporated into each new leaflet: "It needs a clear theme that has been approved at all levels of command. It can be in color or in black and white. Color is more impressive, but more expensive and slower to print. Clear photographs are preferable to cartoons, but both can be used."

The U.S. Army's 4th Psychological Operations Group (Airborne), based at Fort Bragg, North Carolina, designs leaflets at its Media Operations Center and at deployed locations overseas using software like Adobe Illustrator, a popular choice among graphic designers. Leaflets can also be designed in the field as needed.

"Our soldiers are trained in a wide variety of technical skills such as graphic design and layout," says Carol Darby, chief of the media and community relations division of the U.S. Army's Special Operations Command. To ensure that the leaflets accurately communicate their intent, the PSYOP soldiers receive training in foreign languages and cultural awareness.

Opened in 2003, the $8.1-million Media Operations Center at Ft. Bragg houses over 300 military and civilian employees under one roof who handle production, print, distribution and maintenance duties. "The primary mission of the Media Operations Center is to provide strategic and tactical PSYOP support to regional PSYOP battalions," explains Darby.

Alpha Company, which handles printing, has completed orders for millions of leaflets. Next door, Bravo Company, which handles broadcasting, transmits videos and radio programming.

The U.S. Army's psychological operations duties are shared between active duty and reserve units. Approximately one-fourth of the PSYOP units fall under the 4th PSYOP Group (Airborne), while the remaining personnel work for the 2nd and 7th PSYOP Groups of the Army Reserve.

Once they're designed and printed, leaflets are delivered "by military airlift or other [methods] to forward locations where they can be packaged for whatever means of dissemination are required, aerial or otherwise," says Darby. With today's lightning-fast communications systems, "leaflets designed at Ft. Bragg can be sent directly to troops at the front," adds Friedman.

**Delivery: from cardboard boxes to robot parachutes**

Which aircraft can carry leaflets? "What have you got?" answers Friedman. "During Vietnam we used mostly Cessna O-2 Skymasters and Douglas C-47s. Since then just about all combat aircraft can drop leaflets if needed." Even the venerable Boeing B-52 bomber has delivered leaflets over enemy territory. In Iraq and Afghanistan, coalition forces used such widely varied aircraft as the C-130 Hercules and its variants, Boeing F/A-18 Hornet fighters and Sikorsky UH-60 Blackhawk helicopters.

Military leaflet-dropping operations are as old as manned flight itself, dating back to the early days of ballooning. Later, with airplane technology in its infancy, World War I aircrews simply tossed piles of leaflets overboard, either by hand or enclosed in a sack. During World War II, American forces adopted techniques learned from the Royal Air Force, delivering leaflets from bombers traveling over enemy-held territory in Europe. Over time, better ideas ensured more accurate leaflet drops. Newer equipment included tube-like chutes to push leaflets out of the aircraft and boxes rigged with a static line to open them at a prescribed distance.

In the months following the 9/11 attacks, the U.S. Air Force dropped 75 million leaflets across Afghanistan, promising a £12.6 million (US$25 million) reward for the capture of Osama Bin Laden. The leaflets were delivered by the M129 "leaflet bomb," a fiberglass canister outfitted with a time-delay fuse that separates the device into two halves, scattering its contents into the air. The M129 can carry between 30,000 to 80,000 leaflets depending on size. Typically the leaflets are on rolls over a foot (0.3m) in diameter, placed side-by-side in the canister.

A familiar system since the Vietnam War, the M129 is gradually being phased out, with newer dispensers like the PDU-5/B taking its place. In November 2001, the Air Force Information Warfare Battlelab at Lackland Air Force Base, Texas, modified a Mk-20 Rockeye II cluster bomb canister to carry leaflets. The newly christened PDU-5/B leaflet delivery system dropped 60,000 leaflets over Baghdad in March 2003, notifying the Iraqi people that coalition forces were on their way to the city. It was the first air strike of the war.

In addition to "dumb bomb" delivery systems like the M129 and PDU-5/B, high-tech guidance systems like GPS are giving leaflet-dropping a new sense of accuracy. "After all, 50 pounds of the right stuff in the correct place is better than five tons of toilet paper drifting into the wrong place," says Friedman.

A derivative of the Sherpa parafoil delivery system, the CQ-10A SnowGoose unmanned aerial vehicle is the size of a very small automobile and uses a propeller, parachute and GPS to reach its destination. Once there the SnowGoose delivers up to 575 pounds of cargo by ejecting it from six cargo bays in the fuselage at up to six different target areas. To ensure accurate leaflet delivery, SnowGoose recalculates release points while in flight, basing its math on current wind measurements. Once the mission is complete, SnowGoose uses its GPS tracking system to return to home base.

Canadian company MMIST developed SnowGoose for launching from a C-130, Lockheed C-141 or Boeing C-17 aircraft. The device can also be launched from the ground using a HMMWV or a towed trailer. "The SnowGoose has been used by U.S. Special Operations Command in both Operation Iraqi Freedom and Operation Enduring Freedom," says Robert Adam, the SnowGoose program manager. "The Naval Research Lab and the Air National Guard also use the SnowGoose for payload development testing, disaster relief and aerial re-supply."

Another new system, the CopterBox, uses a special cardboard box and old-fashioned gravity to deliver its cargo. Created by Dropmaster, Inc., an American company based in Fayetteville, North Carolina, the CopterBox is a 32-inch-tall hexagonal cardboard tube capable of carrying up to 60 pounds of cargo. Equipped with a small chute, the CopterBox's three rotor blades autorotate to slow the device's descent. Dropmaster's founder, Chuck Warren, a retired U.S. Army colonel, has touted gravity-powered disposable airdrop vehicles to the Department of Defense since 1998. "They're inexpensive and simple to operate," he says, adding that Army special forces troops have been using CopterBoxes in Afghanistan to drop leaflets. Warren says that his company is currently developing a GPS-guided version of the CopterBox called the Expendable Guided Airdrop Delivery System, or EGADS.

Whatever the delivery system, the use of leaflets in military operations will continue to be an important part of psychological warfare, especially in far-flung regions where computers, mobile phones and satellite linkups are rare or nonexistent. In such places, the old-fashioned approach—a piece of paper printed with a simple message and pictures—can be the most effective communication of all.

# REBIRTH
# OF A
# C-17 GLOBEMASTER

THE GIGANTIC CARGO PLANE DESCENDED onto the 12,000-foot runway in the middle of a dusty, barren plain. The aircraft was a C-17 Globemaster III, the relatively new workhorse of the U.S. Air Force. The wheels touched down on the asphalt, and suddenly the plane began to roll off the runway, striking part of an aircraft arresting system. Veering right, the C-17 then hit a three-foot-high dirt berm. The nose gear collapsed and the right main landing gears were damaged. Finally the airplane ground to a halt, its fuselage resting on the dirt berm and the port wing hanging over the edge of the runway.

Fortunately, none of the crew aboard the C-17 had been injured. The airplane, on the other hand, was in poor shape. The accident rendered it unflyable; the loss of the landing gear had resulted in massive structural damage to the nose and fuselage. Worse yet, the incident had occurred at Bagram Air Base in eastern Afghanistan—right in the middle of a combat zone.

### Rescuing a wounded bird

The C-17 replaced the aging C-141 Starlifter as the primary strategic airlift platform for cargo and troops. The Globemaster can also perform airdrop and aeromedical evacuation missions and is designed to use runways as short as 3,500 feet. Bagram Air Base, site of the C-17 accident, is located in eastern Afghanistan, 25 miles north of the capital city of Kabul. The Air Force unit stationed there provides airlift and close air support for military operations on the ground.

With a Class A mishap (damage estimated at $1 million or more) on his hands and combat missions waiting to use the blocked runway, the base commander at Bagram needed to relocate the crippled C-17 as quickly as possible. Army and Air Force personnel rushed to the aircraft to survey the damage and figure out what to do.

Meanwhile, at the airplane's home station of Charleston Air Force Base, South Carolina, Ken Crumpler received a phone call in the middle of the night. Crumpler, an engineering manager, was responsible for Boeing's field service engineers. "We've had a C-17 incident at Bagram Air Base in Afghanistan," he was told. The date was August 6, 2005. Crumpler immediately got to work.

While the Air Force performs day-to-day operations on the C-17 fleet, Boeing takes care of repairs, supply issues and depot maintenance through its Globemaster III Sustainment Partnership, or GSP. The contract, estimated at $4.9 billion, provides worldwide, round-the-clock support of the 150 C-17 aircraft in the Air Force inventory. Boeing has engineers stationed at Ramstein Air Base in Germany, plus others who rotate through Al Udeid Air Base in Qatar and Incirlik Air Base in Turkey.

Jon Buresh, the GSP program manager, is a former Naval aviator, maintenance officer and 23-year Boeing employee. "We're paid by how well the C-17 fleet performs," he says, "and we'll do whatever it takes to support this aircraft."

And so they did. Within 24 hours of the C-17 accident, Boeing engineers from Ramstein and Charleston traveled to Bagram Air Base to conduct an initial damage survey. Before the week was out a recovery team comprised of five Air Force and 12 Boeing personnel, including Crumpler, arrived at Bagram to assist with the recovery. The Boeing technicians came from the company's Recovery and Modification Services (RAMS) team, trained to assist with rescuing damaged aircraft; while the Air Force personnel were battle damage repair specialists from Charleston and the Warner Robins Air Logistics Center in Warner Robins, Georgia.

Together the military and civilian teams carefully maneuvered the crippled C-17 off the runway using a crane and a flatbed trailer, which served as a wheelchair for the broken landing gear. Because the aft door was unusable due to the tilt of the aircraft, 55,000 pounds of cargo were removed, piece by piece, through the crew door. Engineers clicked together metal airfield matting over the ground to keep their makeshift system from slipping, then nudged the C-17 back onto the runway and over to a parking spot.

**A careful return home**

Next came a fateful question: What should be done with the airplane? The nose had buckled so severely that it looked like one-third of the aircraft would need to be rebuilt. The Air Force considered its options, including scrapping the C-17 outright—a $200 million loss. Crumpler and the Boeing engineers wanted the chance to put the airplane back together.

The only way to repair the C-17 would be to limp it home to its birthplace—the production line at Long Beach, California—where Boeing personnel could patch the fuselage back together properly. It would be expensive, but nowhere near as expensive as replacing the aircraft with another one. Rather than scrap the airplane, the Air Force gave Boeing the go-ahead to rebuild it. "We closed all of the gaping holes and got the aircraft back into shape so it could fly," says Crumpler.

Battling desert winds that raced up to 40 knots (about 46 miles per hour), the Boeing team worked with local military personnel to stabilize the C-17 and identify recovery equipment, tooling and parts that were needed to bring the crippled airplane back to minimal flying status.

Finding the right tools took some ingenuity. "We went to the boneyard, borrowed tooling from the MD-11 (which last rolled off the assembly line in 2000), and modified it for the C-17," says Crumpler. Also adapted for use on the C-17 was specialized tooling that Boeing had previously used to convert passenger liners into cargo planes. Everything was collected and shipped to Bagram.

On October 16th—72 days after the aircraft had fallen off the runway in Afghanistan—the C-17 took to the air, followed by a KC-10 tanker serving as a chase plane. During the next five days an Air Force crew hop-scotched the C-17 across the globe: to Al Udeid Air Base in Qatar; the Naval air station at Sigonella, Spain; Lajes Field in the Azores; and finally across the rest of the Atlantic Ocean to its home station, Charleston Air Force Base. There the C-17 was serviced for the final leg of its flight to Long Beach, California.

When the C-17—known to Boeing by its production number, P-96—touched down at Long Beach, technicians were slightly apprehensive but ready to go. Crumpler notes that the GSP program has its own hangar—on the opposite side of the runway from the production line hangar—where Boeing accomplishes minor repairs on C-17s. "But this was not a minor repair," says Crumpler. Technicians were brought in from various Boeing locations across the country to supplement the experts at Long Beach.

**Unbuilding and rebuilding**

The project team held twice-daily meetings to review progress on the damaged jet. "My job was to make sure we had all the right people there as fast as they were needed," says Buresh. "We had to get engineering support and talk to our manufacturing people. We asked ourselves a lot of questions: How do you take out a part? How do you unbuild an aircraft and then rebuild it?"

The first step in the process required gutting a portion of the aircraft. "We took out a 20-foot-long section of underbelly out," Buresh explains. As manufacturing technicians "unbuilt" the fuselage, engineers kept careful watch to ensure that no further damage was inadvertently being done to the nose. Every part removed from the C-17 was laser-leveled to avoid decompression, tension or stress.

During the next 10 months Boeing personnel carefully rebuilt aircraft P-96. Boeing's records reflect the massive undertaking, listing as needing repair the "lower fuselage area, 11 feet by 28 feet; Sta. 227 bulkhead; forward and aft right hand main landing gear assemblies; nose landing gear assembly; and the right hand forward pod." No one had ever attempted a C-17 repair this extensive.

Parts were manufactured as needed, from wherever they were needed. "The biggest major assembly we had to rework was the barrel assembly, a huge underbelly structure that's made in Macon, Georgia," recalls Stan Perez, a modification development specialist who served as a project manager on the project and was tasked with the unenviable job of estimating and tracking the overall budget.

The second major assembly that Boeing had to manufacture was a new right-hand pod to replace the one that crumpled when the C-17 rolled off the runway at Bagram. That part would be assembled in St. Louis, Missouri. "We coordinated with management at two Boeing facilities and worked out a schedule to build these assemblies without interrupting other production flow," explains Perez, a former Navy maintainer with 33 years in the aviation business. "We did the same thing with smaller assemblies like line replaceable units (LRUs)," he adds.

The parts were then shipped to Long Beach, where 53 Boeing employees—technicians, quality inspectors, managers and asset managers—worked two shifts a day, seven days a week, to rebuild the airplane. Air Force oversight came from the local Defense Contract Management Agency (DCMA) office. On the factory floor, P-96 waited as 15 mechanics on each shift flitted around its damaged fuselage. "A lot of folks were moving parts back and forth," describes Perez, "replacing bad ones for good ones." Skin panels, clips, huge assemblies—piece by piece, maintainers accomplished the painstaking work of putting the aircraft back together.

When the repair team had completed its work, the aircraft was repainted in the Air Force's characteristic gray camouflage color. Then it was time to put the aircraft through its paces. To return to the Air Force's active fleet, P-96 had to prove that it was as robust as any brand-new C-17 rolling off the assembly line. Among the tests completed were three check flights to test out the aircraft systems.

**Just like new**

After 10 months, 88,500 manhours and the installation of more than 5,000 parts, Boeing was ready to re-deliver the aircraft to the Air Force. Total cost: $25 million—one-eighth of what it would have cost the Air Force to replace the entire aircraft. Better yet, the complex project finished under budget. "Looking at P-96 today, you wouldn't have a clue what this airplane has been through during the last year and three months," said Buresh at the time. "It was a wise investment for the Air Force."

On November 17, 2006—15 months after the accident—employees at Boeing's Long Beach facility celebrated the rebirth of aircraft P-96. "It looked just like a brand-new aircraft that had just come off the factory floor," says Perez. During the delivery ceremony, the C-17 was unveiled with a new name stenciled on the nose: Spirit of Enduring Freedom.

Lieutenant General Christopher Kelly, commander of Air Mobility Command, the organization accepting the aircraft back into its fleet, attended the ceremony on behalf of the Air Force. "'We can, we must, we will'—you have truly said those things in the craftsmanship and attention to detail, most importantly the grit and determination you showed in bringing back to life P-96," he told the Boeing staff.

The reborn airplane, a phoenix of metal and glass, lived up to its reputation. During its first six weeks back in the lineup, Spirit of Enduring Freedom chalked up a 92.3-percent mission capable rate over 54 missions and 86 sorties. For fiscal year 2007, the airplane scored an 86 percent mission-capable rate, among the best in the C-17 fleet.

In July, Spirit of Enduring Freedom arrived at McChord Air Force Base in Washington to compete in the Air Force's annual Rodeo event, which pits aircraft and their crews in more than 60 competitions. The airplane's owners, the 437th (active duty) and 315th (associate reserve) Airlift Wings, took home the award for Best C-17 Maintenance Team—a fitting tribute to the men and women who maintain the C-17 every day.

Today aircraft P-96 is fondly remembered by the people who spent over a year stitching its fuselage back together. "This project was the most exciting thing in my maintenance career," says Buresh. "We took an aircraft that was going to be scrapped with a forklift and turned it into one of the best-performing aircraft in the fleet."

# BEWARE THE REAPER

IN OCTOBER 2007, A GRAY AIRCRAFT sporting U.S. Air Force markings skimmed across the mountains of Deh Rawod, a district in the Oruzgan province of southern Afghanistan. On command, the plane launched a Hellfire missile, targeting a group of enemy combatants attacking American troops on the ground. The mission was a success, and the aircraft returned to base unharmed.

This was no typical airborne operation. It was the first precision combat strike for a new unmanned hunter-killer aircraft, the MQ-9 Reaper. And while the Reaper flew its mission over Afghanistan, its crew sat at the controls half a world away, at Creech Air Force Base near Las Vegas, Nevada.

At 12 feet tall and 36 feet long, the Reaper is no ordinary aircraft. Labeled "M" for multi-role and "Q" for unmanned, it's a descendant of the original Predator reconnaissance drone and one of the first remote-controlled airplanes to carry live ordnance. Dubbed an Unmanned Combat Aerial Vehicle (UCAV), the Reaper is powered by a single Honeywell TPE331-10GD turboprop engine that propels it at a cruising speed of up to 240 knots (276 miles per hour). The Air Force currently owns approximately 20 Reapers, many of which are assigned to the 42nd Attack Squadron at Creech AFB—the first air combat unit of its kind.

It's been a quick trip from development to deployment for the Reaper, which entered the U.S. Air Force inventory in March 2007. The Air Force accelerated the project so that it could field the aircraft a year ahead of schedule. After that, "it took about 11 months from the time our squadron stood up until its first combat mission," says Lieutenant Colonel Jon Greene, the squadron commander. "We started with two people and now have approximately 100 personnel in the unit."

At approximately $10 million each, the Reapers cost significantly less than traditional manned fighter aircraft like the F-16 ($24 million each) and provide some distinct advantages, including increased loitering time. "We can fly between 12 and 18 hours depending on our fuel state and our ordnance load," says Greene.

According to Tom Cassidy, president of the aircraft systems group at General Atomics Aeronautical Systems, Inc., the San Diego, Calif.-based defense contractor that builds the Predator and Reaper, another advantage of unmanned aerial vehicles is that they typically require less maintenance than manned aircraft. "When you put a lot of time on manned airplanes you have to put them through rework and overhaul at more frequent intervals," he says.

**Into Combat**

General Atomics Aeronautical Systems, Inc. (GA-ASI) launched its unmanned aerial vehicle (UAV) division in the early 1990s. Since then the company has fielded the MQ-1 Predator and the newer MQ-9 Reaper, which is also referred to as the Predator B. Both aircraft are currently in heavy use over Iraq and Afghanistan. "The MQ-1 Predators are dominant over Iraq, but the MQ-9 Reapers are dominant over Afghanistan," says Cassidy. "On any given day there are over 20 Predator series aircraft in the air."

The opium-rich Helmand province in southern Afghanistan was a notorious Taliban stronghold. In November 2007 a Reaper was tasked to provide close-air support to U.S. forces engaged in a firefight with Afghan insurgents in the Sangin district. Fire control was provided by a JTAC, or joint terminal attack controller, operating on the ground. The JTAC sent targeting information to the Reaper crew in Nevada, who launched two GBU-12 laser-guided bombs from the aircraft and destroyed the target.

What's it like to have aircrews in the United States while their aircraft are flying halfway around the world? "It's a unique situation, certainly," says Greene. Because of the limited number of Reapers, for now the 42nd Attack Squadron is responsible for crew training as well as combat missions. "We're training and flying local sorties here at home, and at the same time we're running combat operations overseas," explains Greene.

The three-month training course for Reaper crews—which Greene and his team created from scratch in about four months—graduates its students directly into combat. Traditionally, student pilots graduate from a training unit and are then stationed with an operational squadron somewhere else. In the case of the MQ-9, students train and then fly in the same squadron at Creech AFB.

### Flying the Reaper

Is flying a UAV an entirely different experience from flying a manned aircraft? Not really, says Ed Kimzey, a pilot with GA-ASI. He notes that people often ask if controlling a UAV is like operating a video game. "For the most part it's just like flying a real airplane," he says. "The only difference is that you don't have that seat-of-the-pants feel." Greene agrees, adding that crews "can't feel turbulence, but they can see its effects. You rely primarily on visual cues when flying the Reaper." To keep from getting too comfortable with the technology,

29

Kimzey constantly reminds himself that he's operating 10,000 pounds of aircraft worth over $10 million.

The cockpit of an MQ-9 is given the innocuous label of "ground control station," or GCS. Seated side-by-side in this small room, the two-person crew operates an aircraft that might be cruising in the airspace nearby them or in the skies over another continent. "The ground control station has two pilot racks," says Kimzey, "one for the pilot and one for the sensor operator. It's like a regular cockpit except instead of looking out the window, you look at a television monitor for your outside view." The aircrew isn't limited by location: pilots in portable ground control stations have operated Predators from submarines, trailers and the cargo bays of transport airplanes like the C-130.

Despite its lack of physical feel, the Reaper provides excellent situational awareness for its crew, says Greene, especially at night. Touchscreen monitors in the ground control station provide real-time maps and exterior views. "Even though you're not looking out of a traditional cockpit," says Greene, "you're still able to look at things like a map of all players out there, on the ground and in the air, because of our datalink capability with other aircraft."

To view the environment outside the aircraft, Reaper pilots have three cameras that display their images on monitors in front of them. Two of the cameras—one infrared, the other a color/monochrome daylight TV—are fixed to the nose of the airplane. The third series of cameras provides image-intensified video from a 360-degree rotating pod attached to the Reaper's belly. "You can be five to 10 miles away, up at 20,000 feet, and have a pretty good look at the target," says Greene.

Jason McDermott, GA-ASI's chief pilot, says that with the exception of the TV monitors, the controls are similar to those of a traditional airplane. "When people come out to see the GCS for the first time," notes McDermott, "they often say, 'Oh, it's a real cockpit.'" The pilot flies from the left seat using a joystick controller. To his right, the sensor operator functions as a co-pilot for takeoffs and landings, then oversees equipment like sensors, cameras and weapons. "We still have a stick and throttle," adds Greene, "but we also do a lot of things via keyboard like inputting data for the autopilot system."

As commander of the Air Force's lone MQ-9 squadron, Greene had the distinction of flying the first of his unit's aircraft into Creech AFB in March 2007. Preparing for the flight was no different from conducting mission planning for a manned aircraft like the F-16. (Greene had collected over 3,000 hours in that fighter and was a member of the Thunderbirds demonstration team from 2000 to 2001.) If the Reaper and its crew are co-located, "the crew goes out and preflights it like any airplane," says Greene. "The difference is that we don't physically climb up the ladder and get into the cockpit."

However, when Reapers are sent overseas to countries like Afghanistan, a deployed launch-and-recovery crew takes care of pre- and postflight checks, while the primary aircrew remains at Creech AFB to operate the plane remotely. The deployed crew controls takeoff via a line-of-sight C-band radio signal that transmits from an antenna positioned on the airfield. Once the MQ-9 is in the air, the crew at Creech takes over, controlling the Reaper by a Ku-band satellite link. When the airplane returns to the runway, it's handed back to the deployed crew, which controls the landing.

This procedure is necessary because the Ku-band satellite transmissions include a two-second delay—an acceptable characteristic while the aircraft is in flight or launching munitions that contain their own guidance systems, but potentially hazardous when taking off or landing on a runway on the other side of the planet.

One of the benefits of having the MQ-9's cockpit on the ground is that switching crews is never a problem. "We fly like a multi-crew aircraft," says Chuck Sternberg, the flight operations facilities director at GA-ASI. The MQ-9 uses a crew concept that is similar to that of commercial or military transport aircraft. While the aircraft remains airborne, fresh crews rotate when needed. "The average person in an F-15 would probably last eight or nine hours," he says, and would then return to earth. With the Reaper, "you're not limited by the human factor anymore."

## Testing new technology

In the desert north of Los Angeles, two small airfields bake in the California sun. General Atomics Aeronautical Systems uses these two locations, near the cities of Palmdale and Adelanto, for flight testing and crew training. Live-fire testing is normally conducted at the naval weapons station at China Lake, 150 miles northeast of Los Angeles.

Creating a UAV that could carry weapons was "quite a departure" from the original Predator reconnaissance plane, says Dave Alexander, vice president of engineering at GA-ASI. In the mid-1990s General Atomics Aeronautical Systems began testing a weapons load for the U.S. Air Force by hanging missiles on the MQ-1 Predator. The first ordnance to hang from the MQ-9's wing pylons were the GBU-12 laser-guided bomb and the Hellfire air-to-ground missile.

While the Predator weighs in at 2,300 pounds with a 55-foot wingspan, its newer sibling is over 8,000 pounds heavier with wings stretching over 66 feet. The fuel load was increased sevenfold to 4,000 pounds. Most of the Reaper is built with composite materials.

"The other thing we got away from was single-string failures," adds Alexander. While the Predator contained a single flight computer, the Reaper has three. This system redundancy extends to the control surfaces as well: "If a control surface like an aileron decides to go hard over or limp," explains Alexander, "the rest of the control surfaces can react immediately" to compensate.

## The future of unmanned aircraft

With such a versatile aircraft, it was only a matter of time before other government agencies purchased their own UAVs. The U.S. Department of Homeland Security flies unarmed Predator Bs over the Arizona-Mexico border for reconnaissance purposes and plans to patrol the U.S.-Canadian border with them as well. The National Aeronautics and Space Administration flies a Predator B nicknamed the "Ikhana" (Choctaw for "intelligent") as a scientific testbed. Ikhana demonstrated its versatility when it supplied firefighters with thermal images during the California wildfires of October and November 2007—coincidentally, the same time that Air Force Reapers were flying their first strike missions over Afghanistan.

The Royal Air Force purchased three unarmed Reapers for its 39 Squadron to provide round-the-clock all-weather reconnaissance during combat operations in Afghanistan. As a follow-up, the RAF recently ordered an additional 10 unmanned Reapers in a contract worth over $1 billion. RAF aircrews train and fly alongside U.S. Air Force personnel at Creech AFB in Nevada.

Meanwhile, the U.S. Air Force's 42nd Attack Squadron at Creech is bringing in new crews for training on a regular basis. "It's a growth industry right now," says Greene. "Most new crews coming in are volunteers, and there are plenty of open cockpits for them." The Air Force is expected to order larger quantities of Reapers in the near future.

While the MQ-9 has demonstrated its combat effectiveness over Afghanistan, unmanned aircraft aren't due to replace traditional manned aircraft anytime soon. "The point isn't to replace manned airplanes with UAVs," says Cassidy, "but the UAVs can do certain missions more efficiently than manned airplanes."

"As we enter a new era of unmanned flight," says Greene, "it's a privilege to be in on the ground floor."

# WINGS
# IN THE PAST

# THE BAT BOMBS
# OF WORLD WAR II

IMAGINE THOUSANDS OF BATS — silent, gray-furred, vigilant — huddled in the rafters of your home or office, each carrying a tiny device no larger than a thimble. Suddenly the devices explode, one after the other, engulfing everything — walls, doors, windows, floors — in a ball of flame. In a matter of minutes, entire buildings are incinerated, leaving behind scatterings of charred wood and piles of ash.

While this description sounds torn from the pages of a science fiction novel, it's closer to reality than one might think. During World War II, a quirky inventor proposed that one million bats be gathered from caves in Texas, strapped with napalm incendiaries, and packed a thousand at a time into cluster-like bombs. Dropped from American aircraft over Japan, the bombs would fall to a predetermined altitude, then release the bats to roost in the paper-and-wood buildings below. A timing device would trigger the bombs, setting the napalm aflame — and entire cities ablaze.

One man was daring enough to suggest this scenario to the U.S. government in 1942. Lytle "Doc" Adams was neither a chemist nor an expert in ordnance. He was a dental surgeon and part-time inventor from Irwin, Pennsylvania. When he wasn't poring over mouthfuls of teeth, Adams was perched at a drawing board, generating concepts both wild and practical. Writing in the April 1988 issue of *Technology and Culture*, William Trimble and W. David Lewis said of the fiery dentist, "Adams was a self-styled inventor who saw technology as a means of adding to the common weal and invention as most useful when it could be made available to the majority of the American people." At the 1934 Century of Progress Exposition in Chicago, Adams demonstrated an airborne mechanism that picked up and dropped off bags of mail using a ground-based hook-and-cable snaring device. The airplane carrying the mail stayed aloft, never needing to touch the ground.

The advent of World War II sent Doc Adams' imagination into overdrive. He was mulling over how he could contribute to the war effort when a visit to the bat-infested Carlsbad Caverns in New Mexico triggered a fresh idea: "[I] had been tremendously impressed by the bat flight," he later recalled. "Couldn't those millions of bats be fitted with incendiary bombs and dropped from planes? What could be more devastating than such a firebomb attack?"

In mid-January 1942, Adams fired off a letter to President Franklin Roosevelt. "Dear Mr. President," wrote Adams, "I attach hereto a proposal designed to frighten, demoralize, and excite the prejudices of the people of the Japanese Empire." Outlining what he called a "practical, inexpensive, and effective plan," Adams theorized that airplanes could carry millions of the winged "fire starters" to their targets. An interested President Roosevelt pegged the concept as worth pursuing. In an interagency memorandum, he wrote, "This man is *not* a nut. It sounds like a perfectly wild idea but is worth looking into." The government's interest in Adams' seemingly cockamamie idea was not surprising: after all, the same government was researching pigeon-controlled missiles and bombs triggered by atomic chain-reactions. In the heat of wartime, anything that sounded even halfway feasible was taken under advisement.

After due consideration, the government green-lighted the project and assigned oversight duties to the U.S. Army Air Forces. Doc Adams swiftly assembled a rag-tag team of researchers that rivaled any group of comic-book heroes. In addition to Dr. Jack von Bloeker, a mammalogist from the Los Angeles County Museum, there was a pilot-slash-movie actor, 24-year-old Lieutenant Tim Holt; the brothers Bobby and Eddie Herrold, an ex-hotel manager and workout king, respectively; driver and ex-gangster Patricio "Patsy" Batista, who claimed to have worked for Al Capone; another set of brothers, the unassuming Frank and Mark Benish; and Ray Williams, a lobster fisherman turned U.S. Marine. Rounding out this odd group were two high school student assistants from von Bloeker's laboratory, Jack Couffer and Harry Fletcher. Most of the team members were enlisted into the Air Force for the duration of the project. Adams, well aware of the prestige and political value of military rank, unilaterally promoted many of his team to "acting" noncommissioned officer status. Harvard chemist Dr. Theodore Fieser, the inventor of napalm, would join the team later.

Adams' hiring practices were as eccentric as the man himself. Scientists like von Bloeker and Fieser, assistants like Fletcher and Couffer — these selections made perfect sense from a research perspective. But what about the lobster fisherman and the mafia wheelman? "I think Doc Adams picked them because he felt that they would be loyal to him," recalled Jack Couffer. "He chose them more for personality than technical expertise. It was a very oddball team." Couffer, who would later write about the project in his 1992 book *Bat Bomb*, remembered Adams as "a very appealing character. He was always happy, always jolly, and able to talk to anybody and immediately engage them. He could talk to some old desert rat as quickly as a major general and win him over. That's why I think he succeeded in getting anybody to listen to his crazy idea."

Couffer's introduction to Doc Adams and the bat bomb project was pure Hollywood: "Adams untied a frayed rope from around a worn-out leather briefcase and dove into the interior. He pulled forth a document and flashed its red stamped notice with the word 'Secret' conspicuously emblazoned in the margin. 'Can't let you read this,' he mumbled, implying far more textual content than there was, 'but it's my letter of authority from the Great Man himself.'" While the President's communiqué was impressive, Couffer also knew that with the war underway and his eighteenth birthday approaching, he would soon be drafted for military service. Why not, he thought, contribute to the war effort by participating in a covert government project? So he did.

Doc Adams' team plunged headfirst into their research, tackling a tricky series of challenges on their way to constructing a functional bat bomb. The bats would need to be chilled to force them into hibernation as they were transported by airplane to the target area, then awoken just in time to swoop down into the enemy cities before their time-triggered bombs detonated. Basic questions begged for answers: How far? How fast? How cold? And what kind of miniature bomb would fit on a bat?

At first glance, attaching tiny incendiary devices to bats might seem abusive. But in the climate of the time, sacrifice was paramount, and the bats were needed for the war effort. "The idea of killing a million bats wouldn't fly very far today," acknowledged Couffer, "and it wouldn't have flown very far back then, except for those extraordinary circumstances. It was a time when the war meant everything, and everyone was involved in it one way or another." Couffer added that Doc Adams' research team felt the loss more acutely than anyone else, but realized that "a million bat bombs could save a million lives."

After rigorously testing several species, Adams and his crew settled on the Mexican free-tailed bat to carry their incendiaries. Largely concentrated in New Mexico and Texas, the free-tailed bat population numbered variously from 50 to 100 million. Nearly nine million of them were thought to reside in Carlsbad Caverns, New Mexico, the original inspiration for Adams' bat bomb concept. Since the Caverns were located in territory overseen by the National

Park Service, Adams received special permission to venture into the caves and harvest large batches of the creatures.

Back at the team's laboratory, Dr. Fieser replaced the original incendiary, white phosphorus, with his own invention, napalm. Both incendiaries were highly volatile. White phosphorus sparked into flame upon contact with oxygen. Napalm, a jellied gasoline, was safer to handle and burned more coolly than white phosphorus. Tests demonstrated that the half-ounce bats could each carry between 15 and 18 grams of payload. Using Adams' initial notes, Fieser fashioned a napalm-filled cellulose capsule that he called the H-2 unit. "The incendiary was little, about as big as my forefinger to the second joint," noted Jack Couffer.

Next came an altogether different issue: how would each bat wear its bomb? After experimenting with different options, the team settled on a simple tactic: use an adhesive to glue the incendiary to the bat's breast. The bomb carrier, a five-foot-long sheet metal tube, held 1040 bats in 26 round trays each approximately 30 inches in diameter. As Couffer recalled, "We then loaded what we called the 'armed bats' into the bomb carrier, which was like putting eggs into an egg crate and closing it up." During bomb drops, the bomb carrier would plummet to an altitude of 4,000 feet and shoot up a parachute, slowing its descent as the sides blew apart and the bats fluttered out to descend on the enemy city below.

Theory was interesting, but the military wanted hard results. Dr. Fieser penned a report that ballparked how real-world bat bombing missions would fare. According to Fieser, while standard incendiaries might produce up to 400 ground fires on a single mission, bat bombs could ignite nearly 4800 — a twelve-fold increase in destructive power. Unfortunately, progress in the bat bomb project was marred by less-than-spectacular trial demonstrations at Muroc Lake, California. Over 6,000 bats participated in the Army-sponsored assessments. During simulations involving the use of non-flammable dummy bombs, some of the bats failed to wake from hibernation and fell to earth; others chose to fly away into the sunset, never to be seen again. Later, at the brand-new Carlsbad auxiliary airfield, the accidental release of six live-loaded bats burned the base to the ground. Adams' team had better luck during a later test, as bomb-laden bats successfully destroyed a simulated Japanese village. All things considered, even accidental detonations proved the effectiveness of the bat bomb in destroying targets. Now Doc Adams' team needed to prove that the bats could be controlled.

Unsure of the bat bomb's value and stymied in bureaucratic taffy, the Air Force washed its hands of the project in 1943. An undaunted Doc Adams opened fire, chatting up everyone within earshot, desperate to keep his project going. At the urging of a Marine Corps officer who observed the tests, the U.S. Navy picked up the venture, labeled it with the sinister codename "Project X-Ray," and assigned it to the Marines for further research. That December, Doc Adams' team watched as their bats ignited multiple simulated fires at the Dugway Proving Ground outside of Salt Lake City, Utah. More testing was planned, followed by a production start date in May 1944, when one million incendiary devices would be created. After two years and two million dollars in research costs, the bat bombs would be ready to go to war.

But behind the scenes, another military experiment was about to speed right past the bat bomb project. After a trip to D.C., a baffled Doc Adams remarked to his team, "Some general I met regarding appropriations confused our secret project with another secret project that's apparently going on somewhere. It's the silliest nonsense you ever heard of." That "nonsense" was the A-bomb research underway at Los Alamos, New Mexico. Years later, Jack Couffer mused that "there was no point in fiddling with bats when they had something like the atomic bomb." The Navy cancelled Project X-Ray in late 1944.

As the war progressed, the notion of using incendiaries to torch enemy cities continued on but in different form. American forces kicked off a series of firebombing raids on the Japanese mainland in March 1945. In his book *Laboratory Warriors*, Tom Shachtman painted a dramatic picture of the effects of an Allied firebombing raid on the Japanese mainland: "Three hundred bombers dropped 2000 'jellied gasoline' incendiaries on Tokyo on March 9, 1945, specifically targeting the densely populated area of Shitamachi, with its lath-and-clapboard buildings and small 'shadow factories' that performed subcontract work for Japanese armaments firms. The resultant firestorm was larger than Dresden, consuming 16 square miles and killing more than 100,000."

Following the war, the members of Lytle Adams' team — research assistant, gangster, lobster fisherman, weightlifter, and the rest — went their separate ways. Jack Couffer, the high school student swept into Project X-Ray, became a successful Hollywood cinematographer, while Doc Adams continued to pursue his lifelong ambition of inventing contraptions to benefit the general public. In 1946, with the backing of the U.S. government, Adams jumped in an airplane and scattered synthetic grass-growing pellets over the Papago Indian Reservation in southern Arizona. His goal? To reseed and reforest tired or burned-out areas. Wrote *Time* magazine, "[Adams] looks forward to the time when his man-made bird-pellets will be used to reseed all Western rangelands every ten years." It wasn't as crazy or exotic an idea as the bat bomb — but then, what could be?

# THE BOMBING OF BLY

SPINNING SHARDS OF METAL ripped into the tall pine trees, burrowing holes into bark and ripping needles from branches. The nerve-shattering crack of the exploding bomb rolled across the mountain landscape. When it was over, a lone figure — Archie Mitchell, a young, bespectacled clergyman — stood over six dead bodies strewn across the scorched earth. One of the victims was Elsie Mitchell, the minister's pregnant wife. The rest were children barely into their teenage years.

On Saturday, May 5, 1945 — three days before the end of World War II in Europe and just three months before the Japanese surrendered — an errant explosive device wreaked its havoc on Bly, Oregon, a tiny logging town 25 miles north of the California state line. Reverend Mitchell, pastor of the Christian Missionary Alliance Church, had invited students from his Sunday school classes to a picnic on Gearhart Mountain in the Fremont National Forest. Everyone piled into the Mitchells' automobile and rode to a secluded area, where Reverend Mitchell dropped off his wife and the other picnickers as he parked the car. Suddenly Elsie called out to him. She and the children had found something on the ground.

"Don't touch that!" shouted Mitchell. He was too late.

"The bodies of Mrs. Mitchell and four of the children were badly mangled from the waist down," the local newspaper would report the next day. "One of the boys had taken the force of the explosion in the head, indicating he may have been leaning over the object when it exploded." At the scene, a horrified Reverend Mitchell stood over his dead wife. Hot shrapnel was still burning on her body. Four of the children — Jay Gifford, Eddie Engen, Dick Patzke and Sherman Shoemaker — lay dead alongside Elsie Mitchell. Joan Patzke, just 13 years old, initially survived the explosion but succumbed to her injuries shortly thereafter.

Forestry workers were running a grader nearby when the force of the explosion blew one of them off the equipment. Another dashed to the nearby telephone office, where Cora Conner was running the town's two-line exchange that day. "He had me place a call to the naval base in nearby Lakeview, the closest military installation to our town," recalls Conner. "He told them that there had been an explosion and people had been killed."

Within 45 minutes a government vehicle roared to a stop in front of the telephone shack. A military intelligence officer scrambled out of the car and joined Conner inside the office. "He warned me not to say anything." Conner says. "I was not to accept any calls except military ones, nor was I allowed to send out any information." The rest of the day proved difficult, as Conner struggled with lumber companies and angry locals who had been stripped of their phone privileges without explanation. Some people congregated outside the telephone office, banging on the windows and doors. A frightened Conner handled it as best she could. "After all," she says, "I was only 16 years old." Ironically, Conner had narrowly missed becoming another victim of the balloon bomb. "Dick and Joan Patzke were in our kitchen that morning and invited my sister and me to join them on the picnic," Conner recalls. "But Saturday was a workday in our house, so we didn't go."

Back on the mountain, Army intelligence officers joined the local sheriff at the accident site. The bodies of the victims were grouped within a 10-foot radius of the explosion, which had churned up the forest floor. At the center of the impact zone, seated on a snow pile six inches deep, were the rusting remains of a bomb. A huge paper balloon, deflated and pockmarked with mildew, lay nearby. To disarm the weapon, a bomb disposal officer had to render safe four incendiary bombs, a demolition charge, a flash bomb and a number of blowout plugs.

The U.S. government immediately shrouded the event in secrecy, labeling the six deaths as occurring from an "unannounced cause." But in the close-knit atmosphere of Bly, many of the locals had already learned the truth: Elsie Mitchell and the five children were victims of an enemy "balloon bomb," held aloft by a gigantic hydrogen-filled sphere and whisked from Japan to the western seaboard of the United States. The contraption had alighted on Gearhart Mountain, where it lay in wait until the fateful day when it found its victims — the only deaths from enemy attack within the United States during World War II.

The Japanese high command launched balloon bombs against the United States for a period of six months, from November 1944 through the spring of 1945. In an ironic twist, the Japanese had canceled the program just several weeks prior to the incident in Bly, citing the program's apparent ineffectiveness. A five-month media blackout ordered by the U.S. government helped disguise the fact that several hundred Japanese balloon bombs *had* reached the West Coast. Woodsmen in Spokane, Washington, stumbled across two fallen bombs on the ground and, according to reports, "fiddled" with the devices, which failed to detonate. Elsewhere, a farmer noticed one of the balloons drifting in the sky above, then watched as it plummeted to the ground and wedged itself against a barbed wire fence. He was able to secure the device for investigation by the FBI and military authorities. Week after week, the public reported more and more sightings of the mysterious airborne devices. Balloons fell into rivers, tumbled onto forest roads, and interrupted electric service when they dropped onto power lines. Military pilots engaged balloons in midair and shot them down.

For Americans living near the coastline, the threat of a Japanese invasion by air or sea was nothing new. In September 1942, a Japanese submarine surfaced off the Oregon coast and launched a small airplane that dropped a 165-pound incendiary bomb load over the Siskiyou National Forest. Authorities quickly contained the resulting fire, which was minor and had little effect. Further exploring their long-range options, the Japanese military also planned to riddle the American coastline with submarine-fired rocket volleys. But as the war continued and the Allies marched ever closer to Tokyo, the Japanese high command altered its plans. The balloon bomb, though seemingly a passive weapon, provided the Japanese with an effective method of bringing the war to American shores without expending enormous amounts of manpower and materiel. When detonated, the balloon bombs could trigger massive forest fires in the northwestern United States that would divert manpower from the war effort and knock the lumber industry back on its heels. Moreover, the potential devastation would hammer away at American morale.

The Japanese balloon project was revenge for an altogether different morale-smashing mission. Back in April 1942, four months after the Pearl Harbor attack, Lt. Col. Jimmy Doolittle and his sixteen B-25 medium bombers roared off the deck of the aircraft carrier U.S.S. *Hornet* to pummel targets in and around Tokyo. While hardly a win-the-war mission, the Doolittle Raid was an effective psychological ploy, proving that American forces had the capability to strike the Japanese homeland. In retaliation, the Japanese high command injected new life into its previously dormant balloon project, which had begun in the early 1930s but was relegated to the back burner as other wartime priorities took hold.

Two years passed before the Japanese launched the first operational balloon bomb across the Pacific. Although the designers planned to have the balloons drop their ordnance via time fuse, a more important question had to be answered: how would the device maintain altitude for 70 hours as it traversed 6000 miles of ocean? Some sort of altimeter was needed to respond to changes in air pressure as the balloon sailed along its path. A gas-discharge valve and ballast-dropping system were added to the design, allowing the balloon to self-correct any drops in altitude. The jet stream — an atmospheric phenomenon just beginning to be understood — would do the rest, carrying the balloon from the Japanese mainland all the way to North America.

The Japanese set a production goal of 10,000 balloons. Due to wartime shortages, only 300 balloons of rubberized silk were crafted; the rest were made of paper. Schoolchildren were drafted to paste together balloons in seven factories around Tokyo. When pumped full of hydrogen, the spheres grew to 33 feet in diameter. Each balloon was wrapped in a cloth band from which hung a set of 50-foot shroud lines to carry its ordnance and instruments. A typical balloon was equipped with five bombs, including a 33-pound antipersonnel device and several types of incendiaries. To launch the weapons en masse, the Japanese selected three sites on the island of Honshu. Each launch procedure required 30 personnel and took half an hour to complete. With good weather, several hundred balloons could be launched each day.

After several hundred tests, the Japanese released the first balloon bomb — named *fugo*, or "wind-ship weapon" — on November 3, 1944. Additional launches followed in quick succession. A large number of the balloons that reached North America failed to release their bomb loads when they reached their targets. By the summer of 1945, nearly 300 fallen balloons would be found, strewn across 27 different states. In a 1968 treatise about the balloon program in *Air University Review*, Master Sgt. Cornelius Conley noted, "Balloons were reported over an area stretching from the island of Attu to the state of Michigan and from northern Alaska to northern Mexico. This fact points to the greatest weakness in the free balloon as a military weapon: it could not be controlled." The American media reported on many of the earliest recoveries, but in January 1945 the U.S. government's Office of Censorship, hoping to convince the Japanese that their program was failing, ordered a publicity blackout. That same day, a balloon bomb exploded in Medford, Oregon, digging a shallow crater and shooting flames 20 feet into the air.

At first, American authorities surmised that the balloons were originating in German POW camps or Japanese internment camps within the United States. Other experts thought that the devices were weather or barrage balloons that had drifted off course. As more of the balloons were recovered across North America, the military realized that they were dealing with a new type of enemy weapon. With a little scientific detective work, the U.S. government pinpointed the geographical origin of the sand used in the weapons' ballast bags. American B-29 bombers were dispatched to Honshu, Japan, where they destroyed several plants involved in the production of hydrogen for the balloons, effectively crippling the *fugo* project. Back in the United States, military officials quickly coordinated search efforts with forest rangers and law enforcement officials. Airborne coastal defense, less of a priority as the war neared its end, underwent a brief resurgence as the U.S. Army's Project Sunset coordinated radar and aircraft surveillance round the clock. Over 2000 military personnel participated in the overall effort to track, recover and study the balloon bombs.

On May 10, 1945, five days after the bombing of Bly, more than 450 people attended a mass funeral for the victims. Due to the size of the crowd, the service was held at the Klamath Temple in Klamath Falls, 50 miles southwest of Bly. Several Boy Scouts served as pallbearers, as the male victims had all been members of the local troop. To help avoid similar tragedies from occurring, the government lifted its media blackout. In late May 1945 the headquarters of Western Defense Command, based at the Presidio of San Francisco, issued a cautious message entitled "Japanese Balloon Information Bulletin No. 1." In an effort to avoid a media frenzy and quell public paranoia, the document was to be read aloud to small gatherings "such as school children assembled in groups, preferably not more than 50 in a group and Boy Scout troops." The bulletin warned that "many hundreds" of Japanese balloons were reaching U.S. and Canadian airspace. If anyone came upon a balloon bomb on the ground, the document instructed him or her to keep at least 100 yards away from the device and inform the local police or sheriff. "Let us all shoulder this very minor war load," read the bulletin, "in such a way that our fighting soldiers at the front will be proud of us."

In Japan, radio broadcasts trumpeted the success of the balloon bomb program, claiming that the devices had triggered major fires and caused 500 American casualties. The propaganda broadcasts promised that Japanese soldiers would invade the United States by the millions, all carried to the enemy coast by massive balloons. In reality the Japanese high command had heard little about the balloon bombs' effects on the United States and abruptly cancelled the program in April 1945. Of the 9000 balloons launched by the Japanese, experts estimated that perhaps 900 reached North America.

The accident site in Bly became a tragic landmark for the local community. In 1950, the Weyerhaeuser lumber company asked Robert Anderson, a local stonemason and Navy veteran, to create a monument to the victims of the Bly balloon bomb. A newspaper account noted that "the wooded spot where tall pines show scars left by bomb fragments has been set aside by Weyerhaeuser Timber Company as Mitchell Recreation area, named in honor of the Rev. Archie Mitchell, sole survivor of the war tragedy. The location is on a Weyerhaeuser tree farm." Today the land is supervised by the Forest Service.

Though the town of Bly soldiered on, the shock of the balloon bomb incident reverberated for decades afterward. Some 40 years after the deaths on Gearhart Mountain, John Takeshita, a former resident of the wartime U.S. relocation camp at Tule Lake, California, met a Japanese woman who as a young student during World War II had pieced together paper balloons in Tokyo. Takeshita, intrigued, talked to the woman and many of her former classmates — all unwitting participants in the balloon project during the war — and shared the story of the tragedy that had occurred in Bly. In 1985 the Japanese women crafted 1000 paper cranes — symbols of peace — and sent them to the family members of those who were killed by the balloon bomb. Later, handmade dolls and handwritten letters arrived from Japan, each one a heartfelt apology to the people of Bly.

In May 1995 — fifty years after the incident — nearly 500 people convened in the Mitchell Recreation Area for a rededication of the accident site. "It was really something," remembered Ed Patzke, brother to two of the victims. "Hard to believe it could be put on by a little place like this. They had 10 big school buses to transport people to the site. There were several different speakers. They were playing taps and the bagpipes played 'Amazing Grace.' Near the end they had a flyover by the fighter jets from the Air National Guard unit at Kingsley Field. Most of the town was there. It was very effective." John Takeshita purchased cherry trees to plant at the accident site, at Reverend Mitchell's old church in Bly, and at a school in Japan that had supplied students for the balloon project.

On the day of the rededication, Cora Conner was finally able to come to terms with what had happened on Gearhart Mountain half a century earlier. Locked away in the telephone office on the day of the bombing, unable to inform anyone about what had happened, Conner was haunted by the incident long after the bodies were cleared away. "I had really, really bad nightmares for years," she says. "I didn't realize what was causing them until I met John Takeshita and the Japanese women who visited Bly for the ceremony. One of the girls who had been involved in making the paper for the balloons was the same age I was. I was fortunate to meet her and talk about what had happened. It began to ease the pain, and eventually the nightmares stopped."

For the Reverend Archie Mitchell, who lost his wife, unborn child, and five members of his church on that fateful day in 1945, life eventually resumed its course. He later remarried and in 1947 moved to Southeast Asia to continue performing the missionary work that inspired him. Unfortunately, fate would deal him yet another blow. On June 1, 1962, a tragic wire report brought his name back into the news: "Today word came from South Vietnam that three Americans had been kidnapped by Communist guerrillas. One of them is Reverend Archie E. Mitchell, a former pastor at Bly in southeast Oregon." Reverend Mitchell was never heard from again.

Even today, unrecovered balloon bombs are thought to dot the North American landscape — bombs that are slowly disintegrating with time but

52

are still potentially lethal. To date, approximately 300 of the aged weapons have been found. As late as 1992, a balloon bomb was recovered in Jackson County, Oregon, about 100 miles west of Bly, where the community continues to keep vigil over the forest memorial to the six victims of the World War II tragedy. Nearby, the Klamath County Museum keeps the history of the incident alive for current and future generations. Todd Kepple, manager of the museum, notes, "It's safe to say that we'll always feature an exhibit on Japan's balloon bomb campaign, including its general failure to inflict the widespread damage that was intended, and the heartache it caused in one tiny Northwest community. Many current residents of southern Oregon are scarcely aware of the history of Japanese balloon bombs, but a handful of local residents are determined to make sure the story is never forgotten."

# A TRIBUTE TO WWII AIRMEN:
## *TWELVE O'CLOCK HIGH*
### THE EVOLUTION
### OF THE MOTION PICTURE

A HARD-HITTING NOVEL THAT INSPIRED a classic war film, *12 O'Clock High* was a very personal project for co-authors Beirne Lay, Jr., and Sy Bartlett. Drawing from their experiences as Eighth Air Force officers during World War II, Lay and Bartlett crafted a heady mix of combat heroics and interpersonal drama primarily based on the exploits of the 306th Bombardment Group, one of the first American units sent to England to battle for air supremacy in the European Theater. The resulting novel and film boasted an authentic grittiness that only true life could inspire.

Ironically, the project almost didn't get off the ground. At the end of the war, Bartlett tried to convince his friend Lay that a novel would serve as a powerful historical record and an equally good motion picture. Lay, a writer and pilot who had served as a bomb group commander, wouldn't agree to such an emotional project so soon after the last shot had been fired, feeling that it was too soon to write a book, and too late to make a film. "The time just isn't right," Lay told his friend. "People are tired of war films." But the enthusiastic Bartlett finally coaxed Lay into agreeing, and the two men got to work.

At the time Lay was sharing a small apartment with relatives in Los Angeles, California. Unable to work in such cramped quarters, he turned the basement of the building into a makeshift office. "Once I had seated myself at the orange crate which served as a desk for my portable [typewriter], illuminated by a naked ceiling bulb and a small cellar window on one wall, I was on my own. There was nothing else to do but write." For the next 15 months, Lay and Bartlett crafted a tale of a bomb group commander, Brig. Gen. Frank Savage, whose hard-charging leadership boosted his unit's combat performance but ultimately overwhelmed him psychologically. Bartlett had returned to his prewar civilian career as a writer-producer at Twentieth Century-Fox studios, so he would get together with Lay in the evenings. Credit for the book's title went to actress Ellen Drew, who was married to Bartlett at the time. According to Lay, "She overheard us discussing German fighter tactics, which usually involved head-on attacks from 'twelve o'clock high.' 'There's your title!' she cried." Harper Brothers publishers rolled out the first hardcover edition of *12 O'Clock High* in the spring of 1948.

The real-life inspiration for *12 O'Clock High*, the 306th Bombardment Group, served in combat from October 1942 until April 1945. Nicknamed "The Reich Wreckers," the unit was based in the village of Thurleigh, 30 miles west of Cambridge, England. During its early forays against enemy targets, the 306th suffered heavy casualties. "We were averaging 10 percent losses" on each mission, noted Bill Lanford, one of the pilots. "Not a happy thought for those that hoped to complete a 25-raid combat tour." In seven months, the 306th lost 20 of its original 35 crews in addition to several replacement crews. Bomber Command held the group commander, Col. Charles "Chip" Overacker, responsible for his unit's weak results. Part of the problem was

Overacker's growing commitment to his troops. He was a social man who cherished close relationships, a characteristic that made him more of a father figure than a hardnosed combat leader. Up at Headquarters VIII Bomber Command, Brig. Gen. Ira Eaker grew more and more concerned with the 306th's performance.

To be fair, early tasking orders were hindered by the headquarters staff's lack of experience at planning major bombing operations. Jack Ryan, a member of the 306th, pinpointed several problems with early Eighth Air Force bombing missions: "lack of combat experience at all levels of command and lack of a bombardment tactical doctrine" -- and a seasoned enemy. "We faced a Luftwaffe bloodied in the Spanish Civil War and during three years of combat on two fronts." The American aircrews, by contrast, had to learn by doing. "The lessons from those early missions were learned at the cost of staggering losses," recounted Ryan. But results were most important, and according to James Parton, who served on the Eighth Air Force headquarters staff, "the group's record, measured by number of bombs on target and by B-17s lost, became the worst in VIII Bomber Command." And so, on 4 January 1943, Eaker replaced Overacker with someone he hoped would overhaul the 306th Bombardment Group: Col. Frank Armstrong.

In *12 O'Clock High*, Beirne Lay and Sy Bartlett modeled much of their central character of Brig. Gen. Frank Savage on Armstrong, an expert at bombing operations who had joined the fledgling Army Air Corps in 1928 and led the first American heavy bombing mission into occupied Europe during World War II. According to Donald Bevan, a B-17 waist gunner in the 306th Bomb Group, "Armstrong was a strong, leading man type, with Hollywood flair of dress." He commanded the 306th from 4 January through 17 February 1943. Despite the group's poor reputation with Bomber Command, Armstrong privately thought of the 306th as "a sharp outfit with an excellent record." As an interim leader, Armstrong brought the unit out of the doldrums. "Frank Armstrong was the kind of tough leader that was needed to turn the situation around," remembered John Lambert, a pilot with the 306th, "and that is exactly what happened as a natural consequence of his taking command in January of 1943. I do not remember any one thing that he did to get these results. He was just a good combat commander who inspired confidence and, to a man, the group quickly shaped up under his leadership."

A key plot point in *12 O'Clock High* was Gen. Savage's mental "crack-up": overwhelmed, unable to deal effectively with the repeated losses of men to the enemy, Savage collapsed under the strain. During World War II, in addition to creating a daylight bombing strategy from scratch, the Eighth Air Force had to map its way through uncharted psychological territory. How would aircrews react to combat, and what was the best way to deal with it? The medical community had to treat not only physical wounds, but also unfamiliar mental conditions that crewmen suffered during the war. These problems ranged from exhaustion to breakdowns like the one Gen. Savage experienced in *12 O'Clock High*. "When a flyer was undone by missions," recalled Harry Crosby of the 100th Bomb Group, "when he saw too many planes blow up in front of him, when his tail gunner was cut in two on a mission, when too many of his friends were killed, he sometimes quit. We did not call them 'cowards,' we called them 'combat failures.'"

On a lighter note, Frank Armstrong later wrote that his only regret about the film had to do with Gen. Savage's mental breakdown. Military personnel familiar with *12 O'Clock High* were aware that the character of Savage was based on Armstrong, but not everyone knew that the Savage's psychological breakdown was fictional. "At least a hundred times people who did not serve with us in England asked how long it took me to recover from the breakdown," said Armstrong, slightly miffed. "Those who were there have never ceased to jokingly tell me, 'It's too bad you never quite got over your mental problem!'"

While completing their novel, Beirne Lay and Sy Bartlett also pitched *12 O'Clock High* to film studios, and in 1948, Hollywood gambled on a movie adaptation. Darryl F. Zanuck, studio chief at Twentieth Century-Fox, bought the war story for $100,000, a rather large sum at the time. To recreate a World War II airbase for the film, Fox needed the help of the U.S. Air Force. That September, on the same day he received Bartlett and Lay's draft script for the film, Zanuck leapfrogged the entire military chain of command and wrote directly to Gen. Hoyt S. Vandenberg, the Air Force Chief of Staff. In an enthusiastic and name-dropping letter, Zanuck gently prodded Vandenberg for help: "I do not know whether or not I am a fool to attempt this project at this time. It will call for an investment of approximately $2,000,000 at a time when the national box office has slumped and when most producers are looking for the so-called sure-fire box office entertainment." Zanuck played his cards just right: Vandenberg replied that the Air Force was definitely interested and would assist the studio. A technical advisor, Col. John deRussy, was assigned to the project. He had served as operations officer for Curtis LeMay's 305th Bombardment Group in Chelveston, England, during the war. DeRussy was teaching at the Air Command and Staff school at Maxwell Air Force Base in Montgomery, Alabama, when he received his temporary duty orders for a 90-day assignment on *12 O'Clock High*.

For the film's flying sequences, the Air Force lent the studio 12 B-17 Flying Fortresses with crews, drawing them from Eglin AFB, Brookley AFB near Mobile, Alabama, and other sources. Some of the aircraft had served as drones and drone controllers; others had flown in the 1946 atomic bomb testing program known as Operation Crossroads. Still radioactive, they could be flown only for short periods of time.

At Fox studios, Darryl Zanuck assigned Henry King, an expert at period pieces, to direct *12 O'Clock High*. Sy Bartlett and Beirne Lay revised their script, focusing their story on the difficulties inherent in combat leadership and gradually building up to Gen. Savage's psychological breakdown. Meanwhile, King hopped in his private Beechcraft to scout for locations for the film. A do-it-yourselfer, King noted that he flew "nearly 16,000 miles scouting locations in my usual way, taking my own plane and doing the job personally." With the assistance of technical advisor deRussy, King hop-scotched a number of military installations until he found the right one: Eglin Air Force Base, a sprawling facility of more than 500,000 acres next to Valparaiso and 30 miles east of Pensacola, Florida. Eglin was the proving ground for Air Force and Navy aviation programs and had 10 satellite airfields.

King found the terrain he wanted at Auxiliary Field Number 3, better known as Duke Field, which stood almost 20 miles north of the main base. Duke Field would appear as *12 O'Clock High*'s aerodrome in the fictional English town of Archbury. The studio constructed 15 buildings and packed the set with period aircraft, equipment, and vehicles.

One additional location was required for the film. In March 1949, King and deRussy checked out Ozark Army Air Field, a quiet, weed-infested airstrip near Maxwell AFB in Alabama. King figured that he could use the field for some B-17 aerial shots, but more specifically for the opening and closing scenes of *12 O'Clock High*, when Harvey Stovall visited his old English airbase, now overgrown and fallen into disuse. At Ozark Field, King noted, "weeds had grown as high as a man's shoulders in some places, and the adjacent scenery was perfect as an English countryside." After filming those scenes, the crew would hire mowing machines from local farmers to trim the grass for some B-17 takeoff and landing scenes, as well as a nail-biting belly-landing sequence. Why were two different airfields needed for *12 O'Clock High*? Eglin's runways were light-colored concrete, while Ozark's were black asphalt. To maintain an authentic period look, scenes with airborne aircraft were shot at Ozark because British airfields during World War II had dark-colored runways to camouflage them from enemy eyes.

With filming locations ready to go, Twentieth Century-Fox chartered cargo planes to haul the production crew and its equipment from Hollywood to Florida. Although one might assume that the studio would shoot all the necessary scenes at Maxwell AFB and then move everyone to Eglin (or vice versa), the cast and crew of *12 O'Clock High* actually shuttled between the two bases during the six-week shooting period. Seventy-two members of the production flew on a DC-4 Skymaster from one spot to the other in a short 22 minutes. By car the trip would have taken five hours.

Technical advisor John deRussy secured one million dollars' worth of 1942-era Army Air Force uniforms and gear to use on set. Cocooned in heavy flight clothing, the actors battled the hot, humid Florida environment each day. DeRussy observed the location shooting and came away with a new appreciation of the Hollywood film machine. "I understood why film actors get paid so much," he said. "They work hard!" DeRussy recalled that the production crew worked "fantastic hours" on sets that cost $65,000 per day to operate. Henry King typically allowed the actors one dry-run rehearsal, and then tried to film each scene in one take. Shooting began daily at 8 A.M. and lasted into the evening. "Dailies" -- sequences of recently-shot raw footage -- were reviewed until 8 or 9 P.M.

Twentieth Century-Fox contract player Robert Arthur played Gen. Savage's clerk and driver, Sgt. McIllhenny, in the film. "It was a large cast," recalled Arthur, "and we had been given hundreds of 'dog faces' for background atmosphere." Eglin Air Force Base was a huge facility with a large workforce, so Twentieth Century-Fox was able to use active-duty Air Force personnel as background extras in many scenes. Fresh from basic training, James Storie was at Eglin awaiting his first active-duty assignment when he volunteered for temporary duty with *12 O'Clock High*. "I was an Airman 3rd Class with spare time on my hands. They asked me if I would be interested in helping out in a movie that was being filmed at Field Number 3. I had no idea at that time what kind of movie it was."

Storie reported to the set five days a week for about three weeks, arriving between seven and eight o'clock each morning. "We then lined up at a building and filed through. There was a counter where some person would judge by sight what size clothes we wore. He put our clothes for that day on the counter and told us to don them." After getting dressed, the airmen were led to a holding area until they were called to the set. As for the rank each background player wore, "it was random selection," remembered Storie. "You might be a captain that day, or a private, or anywhere in between." As shooting progressed, Storie came to appreciate the Hollywood actors' laser-like focus on their craft. Gregory Peck, playing Gen. Frank Savage, always knew his lines and rarely needed to complete more than two takes of each scene. The eager extras, on the other hand, weren't as well trained. In the critical scene where Gen. Savage made his fiery introductory speech after taking command of the 918th Bombardment Group, hundreds of airmen playing Savage's crews were crammed into a Quonset hut at Eglin AFB. It took 13 takes to get the scene right. Recalled Storie, "We were dressed in big coats and were given packs of cigarettes to smoke up the room. By the time we finished we were sweating and coughing pretty badly!"

Although the production of *12 O'Clock High* went smoothly, not everything went as planned. Paul Wurtzel, a member of the production staff, remembered an incident in which the filming of the B-17 flying sequences almost caused a tragedy. "They had one shot with a B-17 taking off," said Wurtzel. "They had the camera out in the middle of the runway, and the plane never got up high enough to clear the camera. One of the wheels was retracting. It hit the top of the camera. There were a couple of cameramen out there that shouldn't have been. They should have just turned it on and run away, you know." But they didn't. "The cameramen waited, and the wheel hit a box of filters that was sitting there, and a lot of red filters went up in the air. And they thought this guy got killed. I remember his name as Red Crawford, the camera assistant. After it was over, they went into the NCO Club for a drink or something, and he just fell flat on his face, passed out in a faint. He didn't react 'til a few hours later. He didn't know what had happened to him!"

After initially refusing to provide an operational B-17 for the belly-landing scene, the Air Force relented and instructed technical advisor John deRussy to select one of the aircraft already loaned to the production. Filming of the dangerous belly-landing sequence took place at Ozark Field. It could only be done once: if the scene was unsuccessful, it was doubtful that the Air Force would provide another aircraft for the studio to destroy. Although the Air Force had allowed its pilots to fly the B-17s in formation scenes, it refused to lend any of its crews for the stunt crash. DeRussy, who had personally led some of the formation flying, was eager to belly-land a B-17 but as an active-duty Air Force officer was prohibited from doing so. Stunt pilot Paul Mantz -- who had been hired to film the flying sequences from his camera-equipped B-25 -- volunteered but requested a very high paycheck for the job. When an annoyed Henry King offered to perform the stunt himself, Mantz conceded and settled on a price of $2500.

King set up four cameras to record the shot. According to author Bruce Orriss, Mantz' mechanic loaded the aircraft with minimal fuel and welded a rod across the power switches so that Mantz could cut them as soon as he hit the ground. The studio noted that the scene "called for Mantz to barrel the huge ship between two tents and knock down the poles that were holding them up." Behind the controls of the B-17 *Eager Beaver*, Mantz flew at 110 miles per hour and carefully dropped the 38,000-pound aircraft, wheels-up, on the grass at Ozark Field. It slid almost 1200 feet on its belly and gradually ground to a halt. The nail-biting stunt was quite impressive on screen and would become one of the most memorable scenes in *12 O'Clock High*.

Director Henry King and his company of 150 people completed the four-week location shoot in June 1949. It was time to return to the Fox studios in Hollywood, where craftsmen had built the interior sets for *12 O'Clock High*. These included barracks and offices, as well as the ornate rooms of Wycombe Abbey, the headquarters of Bomber Command. The subsequent five weeks of studio time also involved process shooting in a B-17 mock-up, an abbreviated fuselage modified for camera access. Actors delivered their lines from the mock-up while film of B-17s in formation was projected behind them to simulate flight. Production wrapped on 1 July 1949, and the finished product premiered in December of that year.

A half-century since its creation, *12 O'Clock High* remains a popular and highly respected war film. Still enjoyed by movie buffs and military personnel alike, *12 O'Clock High* has also been used by civilian and government organizations as a leadership training aid. From 1964 to 1967, the ABC network aired a television series based on the film. For actor Robert Arthur, the quality of the project was evident early on: "I think *12 O'Clock High* has withstood the test of time because it is a very fine example of filmmaking. The entire cast and crew was devoted to making a fine example of the spirit of the U.S. Air Force. There wasn't a moment that we weren't determined to make a great movie."

# INVADERS OVER KOREA

*By Frank Moyer, as told to Allan Duffin*

I OFTEN GET ASKED ABOUT MY MILITARY SERVICE and why I stayed for so long. Several influences were of immeasurable help to me: the pride and hopes of my father, of my wife Judy and her family, a Boy Scout background which had inculcated a love and respect for God and country, and a need to earn my own self-respect.

During my World War II service in the Eighth Air Force I was promoted to First Lieutenant. I had been trained to navigate and bomb using the still-secret weapon of radar. Most navigators went over to Europe and came home as Second Lieutenants. I wanted to keep that extra rank—it might come in handy someday.

By early November 1945 I had enough points (credit for combat service and awards) to be separated, so off I went to Lincoln Army Air Field in Nebraska. It was one of the processing centers for discharging troops after the end of the war. I was given the option of a complete discharge or a commission as a First Lieutenant in the Air Force Reserve. It had taken me 26 months as an enlisted man and aviation cadet to earn my commission and several missions over Germany to get my promotion from Second to First Lieutenant. So I accepted the Reserve commission, not really believing that it would ever again lead me into combat. But it did!

American involvement in the Korean war began immediately after the North Koreans invaded the south in June 1950. We all knew we'd be recalled to active duty before long and began to plan accordingly. A composite unit of Reservists from California's 448th and 452d Bomb Wings was activated in August 1950. The unit, designated the 452d Bombardment Wing (Light), had four squadrons of B-26 Invaders. At the time our commander was Brigadier General Luther W. Sweetser, Jr., who had been in charge since the unit's inception in 1949. Not everyone was called up—there were provisions to exempt certain scholars with advanced degrees or personnel who had four dependents, for example. We moved to George AFB in Victorville, California, to train for combat before heading overseas. Quite a few regular Air Force people were brought in to make a complete wing. Our squadron had no permanent armament officer until one of the regulars, 2nd Lt. George Esser, was imported and assigned to us.

In November 1950, one of our squadrons, the 731st, was assigned to Iwakuni, Japan, for night intruder operations in the B-26. The other three squadrons, mine included, stayed together and deployed to Itazuke Air Base in Japan. For the next nine months—one-and-a-half tours—I collected nearly 346 hours in the air over Korea, flying missions constantly plagued by bad weather.

Itazuke was an American fighter base near the city of Fukuoka on Japan's southernmost island of Kyushu. We were based there for about a month before moving to Miho, a former Japanese fighter base on the main island of

Honshu. In May 1951 we moved to K-9, a base just a few miles east of Korea's southern port city of Pusan.

I barely had time to breathe the Japanese air before jumping into combat. I flew my first mission on November 16th, 1950. I had just reached our base at Itazuke the day before. Since none of my flight gear had arrived from our ship, I had to borrow a flight suit and navigation equipment. We were ordered to bomb Namsi-Dong, a North Korean town reputed to hold enemy troops and ordnance. Our only opposition was some small-arms fire. When we returned the bosses gave me a coffee mug with our squadron insignia and my name on it—even though I didn't drink coffee.

On December 4th, I was on my ninth mission, near the south end of the Chosin Reservoir. The 1st Marine Division was spearheading the advance to drive North Korean and Chinese troops back to and across the Yalu River into China. A major influx of thousands of Red Chinese troops nearly trapped the Marines west of the Chosin Reservoir as well as an Army group on the east side of the reservoir. Our four-ship formation bombed, napalmed, rocketed, and strafed Chinese positions in direct support of the Marines. We attacked the enemy within 300 yards of the Marine airstrip there and within 200 yards of our own troops. Because of bad weather we were the only air support they had.

During my 18th mission in January 1951, our four-ship flight made an eight-mile recce (reconnaissance) along the supply routes near Hongchon and hit troop huts with "daisy cutters"—parachute fragmentation bomblets. But low-level work had its hazards. The enemy fired armor-piercing incendiaries that ignited a split second after impact. When we landed and the maintenance crew climbed onto our right wing to refuel us, they showed us where an API round had come up through the fuel tank but didn't ignite until it hit a steel access plate on the top of the wing. It burned a hole perhaps 10 or 11 inches in diameter in the foam rubber padding atop the fuel tank. Had that round ignited when it was supposed to, it would have detonated the fumes in the nearly empty tank, and our airplane probably would have exploded in midair. There's no substitute for luck, is there?

Usually I flew in the right seat of the B-26, but on a February mission I had to ride in the glass nose because we took with us our Turkish pilot, Lt. Muzaffer "Vic" Erdonmez. Vic had come to Korea with the Turkish Brigade. After a short time he joined us for experience in low-level ground support operations. After flying missions with us for awhile, Vic was to serve on the ground as a forward controller of planes supporting ground troops, then return to Turkey as an instructor. He had the darndest habit of getting ready for a mission. The rest of us would be waiting in the barracks for transportation to the flightline, and Vic would wander out of the shower, drying himself, wondering if it was about time to go. Talk about playing it cool! Sadly, Vic wouldn't make it out of our unit: in April 1951 he was on a daylight low level attack mission with our squadron bombardier/navigator, Capt. Joe Farber, when they were shot down and killed.

About a month after Vic's death, our target was the marshalling yards at Chonhwang-Ni, near Kyomi-po. I flew with Bill Tonne and hit the yards from medium altitude, perhaps 8,000 feet. Then we split into three-ship elements and went low-level. We targeted railroad cars two to five miles north of Sariwon and blew them up with two rockets. An enemy rifle bullet shattered the right windshield in front of me. When Bill and I ducked to avoid the flying glass we flew under a telephone wire. The wire sliced through our vertical stabilizer until it hit the main spar and broke it in half. We also got hit on the left wingtip with antiaircraft fire that tore off half its length. We returned safely to our base, but our B-26 was in pretty bad shape.

Night missions were always a challenge. One one trip I flew with a new guy on a road recce from Sinanju to Sinuiju, in MiG Alley. This was my fifth night mission. The taxiways and runways at airfield K-9 were made of PSP, or pierced-steel planking—another new experience for me. We sighted a convoy of about 30 trucks and hit it with 500-pound general-purpose bombs armed with VT (proximity) fuses. When the first bomb hit, 10 or 12 enemy searchlights flashed on to look for us, and I couldn't help thinking of stories from World War II about British bombers over Germany being caught in the lights until the flak guns brought them down. Well, this was the new guy's second or third mission, and he was a little slow to react, I thought. Since I was riding in the glass nose I had great visibility. I directed him through evasive action for perhaps one or two minutes until we escaped the searchlights and headed for home.

I flew my final mission in Korea, number 71, on the Fourth of July 1951. Word had just come down that no one would have to fly beyond 60 missions, but do you think I could beg or buy my way off the flying schedule? Not a chance! And it proved to be a hell of a mission. I flew with Mitchell, a bombardier, and a SHORAN (Short Range Aid to Navigation) operator. It was a very special, new type of mission on which we, as lead ship, would bomb by SHORAN, dropping incendiaries on the target. Then the three planes behind us would drop their bombs on the fires we'd started. But the weather was terrible, and we flew all but 40 minutes' worth in the soup from 8,500 to 11,500 feet. We were getting St. Elmo's Fire—a very bright discharge of static electricity—and in passing very close to Pyongyang we stirred up a lot of enemy flak.

Because of the weather we couldn't get to our target. Worse, the SHORAN set wasn't working, so I couldn't get navigational fixes. We flew into the general vicinity of our recce area (Purple 5, near Huichon) and bombed on my estimate. But on a black night, still in the soup and with no navigational gear, we had to be steered to airfield K-2 at Taegu by TADC (Tactical Air Direction Center). There we broke into the clear and easily found our way home.

Our recall period of 21 months ended in May 1952, and some of our 452nd Wing reservists then returned to civilian life. We were all given the option of leaving or remaining indefinitely on active duty. I decided to stay. Quite a few of us navigators and bombardiers were sent to Mather AFB in Sacramento, California, which was one of two primary navigator training bases at that time. Many reservists and Air National Guardsmen who had just been recalled for Korea were being trained there. Our job was to teach them some of the practical experience we had learned in combat.

At Mather we encountered pronounced differences between regulars and reservists. First of all, many of the regulars had stayed in between wars and, as full-time active-duty types, were the first-class citizens of the Air Force. Since we reservists had gone back to civilian life after World War II, we were therefore second-class. However, none of the regulars at Mather had, of course, been to Korea for any combat. Second, between the wars a new beast had been created: the "Aircraft Observer, Bombardment." All of us reservists were still proudly wearing our WWII aviator wings; the AOBs sported a totally different badge. Some new navigation procedures had been devised during the interwar years, and we knew none of them. The regulars had received electronics training on new postwar equipment; we knew nothing about such mysteries. Little wonder that we were considered, and sometimes treated, like poor country cousins.

But we had our moments! I was working at my desk one day when I was approached by one of the regular officers. He was an instructor for the new navigator and radar navigator classes. He was a Captain; I was still a First Lieutenant. He had made a point in his class that period, and one of his reserve students didn't think it sounded quite right. The instructor asked me, "Is that the way you did it in Korea?" Of course he hadn't been closer to Korea than a weekend in San Francisco. Now he wanted me to come into his class and bail him out—which I did. After that, my fellow reserve instructors were granted a bit more respect.

During the war, the toughest part for my wife Judy was having total responsibility for home and daughters when I went to Korea. We were a Los Angeles Basin group of people, and the wives kept in close touch with one another about all the news that came home from us. Our losses had a major impact on every one of them. The worry factor added a lot to their other responsibilities. But Judy has always been a girl of strong religious faith, and knowing that I would weather my storm enabled her to weather hers. It helped that her dad had served in a machine-gun company during World War I, and had also trained in the Army Reserve prior to World War II, receiving his commission and promotions all the way to the rank of Major. So

Judy's childhood experiences with her father made my service commitments perfectly natural to her in our own family life.

My favorite passage in the Bible is Matthew 5:13-16: "Men do not light a lamp and then put it under a bushel basket. They set it on a stand where it gives light to all in the house.

In the same way, your light must shine before men so that they may see goodness in your acts

..." I've always felt that people can learn something from my experiences and my attitude toward them. I've been called upon to speak before Scout troops, junior chambers of commerce, even a group of model aircraft builders and aviation enthusiasts. If from my experiences folks can gain some insight into dedication to duty, courage, and loyalty to nation, then perhaps I've done some good and sown some seeds which can inform and perhaps even help others. That's my attitude, and I'm stuck with it.

*Frank Moyer began flying when he enlisted in the Army Air Force during World War II. He navigated B-17 and B-26 bombers as well as the EF-105F "Wild Weasel." Moyer was awarded the Distinguished Flying Cross three times: twice for extraordinary achievement in aerial flight and once for heroism. He also received the Silver Star, the third highest award for heroism in combat. Moyer retired as a Lieutenant Colonel in 1969 after twenty-seven years' service.*

# BATTLING CASTRO
# IN A TOWEL

*By James Storie, as told to Allan Duffin*

I'M PROBABLY THE ONLY AIRCRAFT MECHANIC to make an emergency repair while clad only in a towel. But when you're called out from the shower because the airplane on the runway is about to take off on a combat mission, necessity trumps modesty every time.

In early 1961 a friend from my days in the Air National Guard told me that Brig. Gen. George Reid Doster, commander of the 117th Reconnaissance Wing at Birmingham Municipal Airport, wanted to talk to me. I had been out of the Air Guard for five years. Why was the General looking for me?

When I met with him, he laid it on pretty thick. "We have a very important classified mission I'd like you to consider," he said. "That's all I can tell you, other than that you can be of great service to your country." There would be a series of meetings with other people like me who had been contacted for this hush-hush mission.

At the time, few technicians were familiar with the old B-26 bomber—and still fewer were qualified in maintenance and electronics, as I was. Most of the personnel being interviewed were from the Hayes Aircraft company, where I was working at the time; the rest were active Guardsmen. Gen. Doster asked me to make a decision right then and there: did I want to participate? I felt put on the spot, but because I knew most of the guys personally, I was in good company. I took the job.

I knew that the Guard was assisting with this mysterious project, but I wondered who was running the show. Thirty or 40 of us active and former Guardsmen were brought on board one step at a time, with each step taking several days. We used first names only. I was given a picture of a woman and two kids to go in my billfold—I had no idea who they were—along with other documentation.

At first we were given a few broad possibilities about what our mission would be. Those of us who were still interested would have to sign additional secrecy documents. At each step, a candidate remained only if he continued to sign more documents. By then I was pretty sure that we were dealing with the CIA, but this was never acknowledged in the open. We were told how we would be paid and that we could tell no one—repeat, no one—or we would be prosecuted and kept incommunicado for an unknown period of time.

Finally I learned the truth about our mission, and why the Guard needed aircraft technicians so badly: we would be training Cubans to fly converted B-26s for a planned invasion of Cuba, with the goal of triggering a revolution to overthrow Communist dictator Fidel Castro. Since Castro had B-26s in his air force, the theory went, the Cuban population would think that their military was revolting against Castro and join alongside them.

After a week of briefings and paperwork, we were told to report to Eglin Air Force Base near Pensacola, Florida. We left Eglin at midnight in a C-54 with blacked-out windows, flying 50 feet above the water for a very long time. We still did not know where we were going.

The next morning we landed on a dusty airstrip in the middle of nowhere and were told that we had arrived at our base. There was nothing there except the runway. It turned out to be Puerto Cabezas, Nicaragua. Everything was very hush-hush because we didn't want Castro to find out where we were. I was told that the ground troops for the invasion were being trained in Guatemala while we trained B-26 crews at Puerto Cabezas.

The greatest number of B-26s we had at one time was 18, but the count varied since planes would come and go. Where they came from I don't know. I did my job, keeping the planes operable, as training missions took off each day.

After a week to 10 days of practice and preparation, we launched our first bombing mission on the morning of April 15th, 1961. The B-26s, piloted by Cubans we had trained, were tasked to destroy all of Castro's aircraft on the ground, runways and other critical targets, and then provide close air support to the invasion force. The planes had bomb-release capability and lacked gun turrets but did have eight .50-caliber machine guns mounted in the nose.

We had worked all night getting the planes ready. I was finished with my part and left the flight line as the B-26s were starting their engines for takeoff. I headed for the shower tent to wash off the sweat and grime of the previous evening.

I was in the middle of my shower when someone came running after me. "One of the bombers is waiting at the end of the runway and wants you to check their radio now!" he said.

I wrapped a towel around my waist and with shower clogs on my feet rushed out to the runway, where I expected to see a B-26 with its engines shut down. But both propellers were still churning. The crew was worried that if they cut the engines, they might not get them restarted, and would I please try to fix their radio?

The B-26 wasn't nicknamed "The Widow-maker" for nothing. It was a very difficult aircraft to climb into and out of. It was worse if you had to bail out, due to the canopy arrangement and the close positioning of the propellers. I wish someone had a camera that day to take a picture of an idiot—wearing only a towel and shower clogs—climbing up to the cockpit with propellers turning at 1200 RPM only about six to eight inches from him.

I managed to get into the cockpit and have a look at the radio equipment. The Cuban crew was very tense, probably scared, and had a submachine gun lying at their feet. In checking their radios I found a cannon plug that was hanging loose. Once I reconnected it I asked them to try their radio. It worked.

Now I had to get back on the ground. I managed to get down without losing my neck, my towel or my shower clogs. As I stepped down, I don't remember being scared of the propellers just inches away from me. But I don't think I would ever do it again with the engines running like that!

After the first bomb run we were told by Washington to stand down until further notice. It was three days before there was another bomb run, and by then Castro managed to have a Sea Fury fighter-bomber and a T-33 equipped with guns in the air. Our B-26s had no chance against them and they picked and chose as they pleased. It was a turkey shoot.

The Bay of Pigs invasion failed because the air armada wasn't utilized effectively. The whole plan required air superiority. We were supposed to bomb our targets continuously to prevent Castro from having anything to fly—and even if he did, his runways would be so damaged that his aircraft wouldn't be able to take off. All of us knew we had no chance at success after the second bomb run was cancelled.

When we resumed our bombing missions, our Cuban pilots were being shot down steadily. Morale was very low and the Cuban pilots said they would not go back unless some Americans flew with them. There was a big meeting of all American personnel at Puerto Cabezas. We were told about the situation and asked if there was anyone willing to volunteer.

To the best of my memory eight of the American advisors heeded the call. I wasn't one of them. It was not an easy decision for me to make. I declined because as a crew chief on the mission I could do nothing but be another pair of eyes for the pilot and offer moral support. I couldn't see myself sitting there getting shot at, with no way I could help. If I had a mounted machine gun to use, it might have been different. But the only guns on our B-26s were in the nose, and those were controlled by the pilot.

I personally knew all the pilots and crew volunteers except for a gentleman named Joe Shannon. I had flown with Riley Shamburger and Pete Ray at other times and considered Pete a friend. I had worked with all of them at Hayes Aircraft in Birmingham.

On April 19th we launched six B-26s, four of them piloted by American crews. Wade was flying with Shamburger and was the first American to go down. The B-26 piloted by Pete Ray and Leo Baker was the second. Shamburger crashed in the water. Pete went down on land and survived the crash. There was a short gun battle in which Pete was wounded, captured and then executed at the crash site. Only Shannon returned in one piece. The Cuban exiles were unable to sustain the beachhead at the Bay of Pigs and surrendered to Castro's forces.

After the failure of the invasion, we began to close things down at Puerto Cabezas. We were told to turn in our Colt .45 automatic pistols. We could keep the rest of the items we'd been issued, but all of our baggage would be searched at departure. So we left as if we had never been there.

We returned to Florida in the same manner we arrived, on a C-54 minus the blacked-out windows and a good bit more altitude. We were reminded that this was all still top secret and to reveal nothing to anyone about where we had really been or what we had been doing. We were to use the cover stories we were originally given. If any of us felt we were being watched or noticed something unusual going on, we were instructed to contact a particular Air Guard person. Otherwise, we were told to keep quiet and go on with our regular routines.

While I was in Puerto Cabezas a Cuban technician I had been training came to my tent and told me he did not know my real name but he was going to tell me his, and if I was ever in Miami, I should contact him. "I want to give you something," he told me. "It's all I have to give." He presented me with a brand-new G.I. winter coat. I told him how I admired him and would gladly accept it.

Today, more than 50 years after the Bay of Pigs, I still have the coat. I could never tell him who I was, for we were warned that Castro might try to trace us down if our real names were ever known. That Cuban technician was a real hero. I wish I knew what happened to him. At least he knew I cared.

*James Storie served tours in the Naval Reserve (1947-48), Air Force (1948-52) and the Air National Guard (1953-56) before being recalled to military duty to participate in the U.S. government's secret invasion of Cuba during the Kennedy Administration. He lives in Birmingham, Alabama.*

# TRIBUTES
# TO HEROES

# THE MARINE FROM NASA

THIRTY-SIX THOUSAND POUNDS OF EQUIPMENT sits in the payload bay of the space shuttle *Endeavour*. The shuttle — floating more than 200 miles above the earth — eases toward the giant research laboratory known as the International Space Station, then docks gently. Astronauts don their spacesuits and begin spacewalks to connect two new modules to the station: a life support hub and a viewing center.

Inside the shuttle, Colonel George Zamka — the mission commander and a NASA astronaut — guides his crew through the delicate procedure. During this mission *Endeavour* and her crew will circle the earth 217 times, traveling nearly six million miles over the course of 13 days, before returning to earth on February 21, 2010.

The NASA personnel performing this shuttle mission are specially trained. They come from different branches of the military and also from civilian life. George Zamka might be an astronaut, but — like former senator John Glenn, one of the first candidates selected when NASA launched the astronaut program in 1959 — he is also a colonel in the United States Marine Corps.

Zamka's nearly three-decade military career is packed with tremendous accomplishments. He has served as a pilot, racking up more than 5000 hours in over 30 types of aircraft. Out of the cockpit Zamka completed tours as a forward air controller, maintenance officer, and — since his appointment in June 1998 — as one of America's 95 astronauts. To date Zamka has logged nearly 700 hours in space.

### Childhood dreams

Zamka's interest in flight dates back to his childhood. "My mother is from Colombia, and my uncle was a pilot in the Andes Mountains," recalls Zamka. "On one family visit he took us flying. I saw him working the controls and landing on these austere strips in different places. It was very exciting for me, and that's where I got the bug."

By the time he was a senior in high school, Zamka had decided to join the military. "I had been inspired by cadets I saw at West Point, and also had an interest in naval history," he says.

While studying mathematics at the Naval Academy during the early 1980s, Zamka gradually shifted toward a career in the Marine Corps. "I saw some examples of pretty fine Marine officers," Zamka explains. "They influenced me. I thought, 'This is going to challenge me to do the very best I can do.'"

### Into the sky

After graduating from Annapolis in 1984, Zamka trained to fly the A-6E Intruder, a carrier-based attack bomber. Six years later, after cross-training into the F/A-18 Hornet, Zamka would find himself in the middle of a war.

In 1991 Zamka deployed with his squadron to Kuwait. It was the beginning of Desert Storm, and Zamka would soon fly 66 combat missions over enemy positions. His squadron's mission: to act as fast forward air controllers, hunting for targets in the desert that were threats to coalition ground troops. "We were looking for artillery, tanks, and multiple rocket launchers," recalls Zamka.

"Desert Storm was our first major combat in a long time," he continues. "There was a newness to it and a little bit of uncertainty — a sophisticated air threat and a number of unknowns." During a typical mission, F/A-18s would mark the enemy positions with a series of 2.75-inch rockets. Then other coalition aircraft would take out the targets. Depending on the day, the sky could be filled with AV-8B Harriers, Air Force A-10s, Kuwaiti A-4s, Navy aircraft, and additional Marine Corps F/A-18s.

Zamka's squadron typically flew two missions a day. "Sometimes we'd fly one mission in the daytime and the other at night," says Zamka. "Sometimes we'd fly both missions at night." But in the grand scheme of things, he adds, the mission schedule didn't matter. "You got up when the alarm went off. We would get a quick brief, put our flight plan together, then go fly."

After Desert Storm, Zamka briefly served with the First Battalion, Fifth Marines at Camp Pendleton in California. Here, Zamka's experience with forward air control came in handy: After flying FAC missions in the Middle East, he was now performing a similar mission with the Marines on the ground.

Soon thereafter, Zamka was selected to become a test pilot. He spent four years with the Naval Strike Aircraft Test Squadron at Patuxent River, Maryland.

"Test pilots are the translators between the operators and the design engineers," explains Zamka. The most exciting part of the job, he says, was ensuring that a new capability worked the way the Marines needed it to work on the battlefield. Zamka's test missions included flying with an asymmetric (unbalanced) bomb load to make sure that the aircraft remained stable in flight. Some missions even required him to deliberately make the F/A-18 go out of control.

Zamka's background as a forward air controller came in handy during his time as a test pilot. "We did radio checks using new radio configurations," he says. "For FACs on the ground, radios are incredibly important."

Though he says he's fortunate to have spent much of his career flying with Marines, Zamka notes that many people he's met are unaware that the Marine Corps actually has an air component. "When I went to the Air Force test pilot school, people didn't know that Marines had airplanes!" he recalls with a smile.

**Heading into orbit**

In June 1998, Zamka was back in an operational squadron as its maintenance officer when he received a fateful phone call from NASA: he had been selected for the astronaut program.

It would take nine years of training and patience until Zamka got the opportunity to fly into space. In October 2007 he piloted the shuttle *Discovery* as it delivered a new module to the International Space Station.

In February 2009, Zamka served as the mission commander. His crew included a first-time pilot along with four specialists. It was a bittersweet trip: after nearly 30 years of service, the shuttles were flying their last missions, standing down so that a new generation of spacecraft could take their place.

What are the differences between flying a jet aircraft and piloting the space shuttle? The answer boils down to having different targets, says Zamka. "When you're flying in combat, you're going against an adversary," he explains. "There's a dissenting vote — that is, someone coming after you to wreck your plans."

On the other hand, spaceflight features a different type of adversary. "For NASA we are training against a hazard: a hazardous environment. Our enemy is Murphy, as in 'Murphy's Law.' Anything that can go wrong will go wrong."

But once Zamka is flying the mission — whether in an F/A-18 or the space shuttle — the experiences are strikingly similar. "You revert to your training and your habits," says Zamka. "Marines are trained for a bad day."

"We put that training into use in combat," continues Zamka, "to ensure our responses to incoming missiles or artillery are the correct ones." At NASA, the threats are different but the training is just as tough: The astronauts are exposed to simulations — labeled "smart failures" — to train for the worst-case scenario in space.

The "smart failures" pile error upon error to test the astronauts' ability to respond to crises. "The chances of problems lining up exactly that way are very slim," acknowledges Zamka. "But if they do happen, we're prepared. When it comes to actual spaceflight, we're ready to handle even the little things that come up."

Having served on the ground and in the air, Zamka has a unique perspective as a Marine. "I've always been humbled by a Marine and his rifle, and his dedication and courage," says Zamka. "I take those same qualities into space with me: honor, courage, and commitment. Honor to serve the United States in space and to represent the Marine Corps. Courage in counting on your team, counting on your plan, and taking that plan up against the hazards of space. Commitment to doing the best you can — and asking yourself every day if you can do it better."

## Becoming an Astronaut

The National Aeronautics and Space Administration has selected several hundred astronauts out of thousands of applicants since the program began in 1959. How competitive is the program?

To become a **pilot astronaut** — qualified to fly and command the International Space Station as well as the Space Shuttle — candidates must have a bachelor's degree in engineering, biological science, physical science, or mathematics. Also required: At least 1,000 hours of pilot-in-command time in jet aircraft. Test pilots have an advantage. Candidates must also pass the NASA physical, which includes 20/100 or better uncorrected vision and a maximum 140/90 blood pressure. Height restrictions also come into play: candidates must stand between 5'2" and 6'3" tall.

**Mission specialists** control the onboard systems and equipment. They also perform space walks, officially known as extravehicular activities, or EVAs. Requirements include a college degree plus at least three years of professional experience. Vision can be 20/200 or better uncorrected, and height must be between 4'10.5" and 6'4".

**Payload specialists** are non-NASA personnel who join the crews from civilian and foreign organizations. They're typically sponsored by commercial or research firms.

# LEGACY ON A LARGE CANVAS: HBO'S TV MINISERIES *THE PACIFIC*

In 2001, THE HBO TELEVISION CHANNEL unveiled a 10-part docudrama that told the story of World War II in Europe through the eyes of a small group of soldiers from the 101st Airborne Division. Titled *Band of Brothers,*"the miniseries won six Emmy Awards for its detailed depiction of Easy Company from its initial training through the end of the war. Nine years later, HBO premiered *The Pacific,* a companion piece to *Band of Brothers*. Six directors, six writers and a cast of hundreds gathered to tell the interconnected stories of three U.S. Marines during the battles for Guadalcanal, Cape Gloucester, Peleliu, Iwo Jima and Okinawa. *The Pacific* also took a look at how the characters dealt with their return to the United States as combat veterans — and how one of them wouldn't live through the war.

87

The new project was overseen by Hollywood luminaries Tom Hanks, Steven Spielberg and Gary Goetzman — the same group that helmed *Band of Brothers*. Initial planning began soon after *Band of Brothers* made its mark. "[Hanks, Goetzman and Spielberg] called me in the spring of 2003 and we had a meeting to discuss it," says Bruce McKenna, the lead writer on *Band of Brothers* who would serve as a co-executive producer and writer on *The Pacific*.

As with its predecessor, producing *The Pacific* would be a herculean effort. McKenna's first challenge on the project: choosing a cast of characters and plotting their stories. He worked closely with Hugh Ambrose — son of historian Stephen Ambrose, author of the book upon which *Band of Brothers* was based — to develop a database of recollections of Marines who had served in the Pacific. "Hugh and I spent a lot of time together knocking things around and thinking about it, trying to come up with a way of doing the series," explains McKenna. "We decided that we'd pick a variety of guys and weave their stories together, and tell those stories on a large canvas."

### Researching and building a story

To construct a narrative for the series, the production team drew from archival material and books including *Helmet for My Pillow* by Robert Leckie and *With the Old Breed* by Eugene B. Sledge, plus material from *Red Blood, Black Sand* by Chuck Tatum and *China Marine*, also written by Sledge.

Initial research went on for six months, says McKenna. "I realized that a lot of guys who had served with the 1st Marine Division had entered the war early, and then came back to serve on Iwo Jima in the 5th Marine Division. So it became clear to me that if I wanted to tell the entire sweep of the war, it had to be the 1st Marine Division."

With so many Marines in the 1st Division, how did McKenna zero in on the trio of characters he wanted to feature onscreen? "Early on someone recommended that I read Eugene Sledge's memoirs, which I did," says McKenna. "Then I got ahold of Robert Leckie's memoirs. These are some of the best memoirs ever written about combat." As McKenna dug more deeply into the research, he realized that Sledge and Leckie would make terrific main characters in the miniseries.

Next, McKenna needed to find a third character to round out the primary cast. McKenna mulled over his research and found one Marine who fit the bill perfectly: John Basilone, a New York native who received the Medal of Honor for combat on Guadalcanal and was later killed in action on Iwo Jima. "Even though he's famous in the Marine Corps, he's not well known outside of aficionados of the war," explains McKenna. "I thought his story was perfectly emblematic of sacrifice in war that hadn't really been well-told before."

The production team also conducted interviews with dozens of Marine Corps veterans who provided background information along with personal remembrances of Sledge, Leckie and Basilone. "We brought back all of the surviving veterans who had served with our leads and put them on tape," explains McKenna, who eventually had several thousand pages of transcripts stacked on his desk. *Band of Brothers* had required a lot of research, recalls McKenna, but *The Pacific* needed even more.

Finally, McKenna had to connect the three character's stories, building a narrative that would flow smoothly through the 10 episodes of *The Pacific*. Here again, McKenna had a stroke of luck: While interviewing a Marine veteran, McKenna learned that Sledge's best friend, Sid Phillips, had served in Leckie's heavy rifle company on Guadalcanal. "When I found that out," said McKenna, "I knew we had a miniseries."

The three main characters' lives would be interconnected — sometimes directly and sometimes through secondary characters. "We're covering an entire Marine Division that has up to 20,000 people in it," says Dale Dye, a retired Marine Corps Captain who served as senior military advisor on the miniseries. "The difficulty was in constantly moving our story through those three regiments. We had people around those guys whom you got to know. We had to weave through, going from machine guns to mortars to rifles to mortars, and keep the audience with us with recognizable characters at all times," says Dye.

After HBO green-lit the miniseries — with an impressive budget of $200 million — McKenna began another six months of research, this time with a writing staff. "The research never ends," explains McKenna. "We were still doing research even while we were shooting."

The most challenging part of the writing process involved condensing the 1st Marine Division's three-year experience in the Pacific into just 10 hours of television. This required the writing staff to compress the story wherever possible. "The men on Okinawa were there for about 80 days of combat," says McKenna. "We focused on Okinawa for just an hour in the miniseries. I had 55 minutes — a single episode — to distill 80 days of experience. It is daunting — the most difficult thing that [writers] do."

The writers chose specific events to cover, sometimes combining incidents and characters, to ensure that the story wouldn't be confusing to the audience. "You have to figure out what you want to say about the battle," says McKenna. "Sometimes you have to make the hard choice of compressing events and time and characters, to get to the truth of what really happened in that particular battle."

"How do you maintain the integrity of the story of the men you're depicting — who are all real — with the demands and rules of storytelling?" says McKenna. "You can service the truth as well as create a lasting piece of art or entertainment that really moves people."

**Making it authentic**

"We wanted to create the series so that there would be something in there for all of the Marines that would raise gooseflesh on them," notes Dye, "to get them to say, 'Yes, that's how I did it; that's exactly how it was.'" Dye prepared for a year before the miniseries started filming. In addition, he and members of his team had crawled over the battlefields of Guadalcanal, Peleliu and Iwo Jima for an earlier project and were therefore prepared with first-hand knowledge as *The Pacific* began production. Dye's company — Warriors, Inc. — would oversee the training of the cast members, assist directors, coach actors and stage the combat action featured in the miniseries.

Dye and his crew read and re-read the source material, then researched the 1st Marine Division, its structure and tactics prior to August 1941 — when it landed in the Solomons — and afterward. "We were ready to go," says Dye. "We were stocked with some good research. We knew our legacy. We knew our Marine Corps history."

As Dye and his team explored the history of the 1st Marine Division, they uncovered some interesting details. The Division patch, says Dye, was designed after the battle for Guadalcanal and was first produced by a woolens mill in Melbourne, Australia. "When it came out, there was no regulation about how to wear it," says Dye. "The division was wearing Australian battle dress uniforms to replace the American dress uniforms they'd lost during the Solomons campaign. You'll see the patch is sometimes on the left shoulder, and sometimes on the right shoulder." Another historical fact: the Division's official marching song, "Waltzing Matilda," is an Australian tune that was adopted after the Solomons campaign.

Costuming was another area where authenticity was crucial. Penny Rose, costume designer, was helped by the readily available photographic and film documentation of the period — and, like the rest of the production staff, a dedication to making the miniseries as true to life as possible. "You don't mess with it — you do it exactly as it should be," says Rose. To generate enough military and civilian outfits for the actors, Rose shopped in vintage stores and also rented costumes from suppliers.

Maintaining enough authentic uniforms — and backup outfits as well — proved particularly challenging for Rose and her staff. "The uniforms were the greatest challenge because they had to undergo so much activity," explains Rose. "And also, through the series, the uniforms had to get worse and deteriorate."

Television programs like *The Pacific* are usually shot out of sequence: scenes that take place in one area, for example, can all be shot at the same time, which saves on production costs and allows the production to progress more efficiently. Unfortunately, this also means that the costume department had to have uniforms in various states of deterioration — six stages, in fact — ready to go any time. "Since we were shooting the episodes out of sequence, I needed their number 5s and 6s before I needed their number 2s, so we couldn't age the uniforms gradually as we went along," says Rose. "We had to have all six degrees of deterioration ready so we could jump at will."

## A military campaign for the small screen

*The Pacific* went in front of the cameras in August 2007, shooting in the Australian states of Queensland and Victoria. The production would take 10 months to complete. Orchestrating a large cast and crew plus vehicles, equipment and locations was a massive undertaking. "There is a bit of a 'military campaign' aspect to making a miniseries like this," says McKenna.

To build a unit of special ability extras who would interact with the primary members of the cast throughout the miniseries, Dye interviewed between 300 and 350 Australians who would portray members of the 1st Marine Division. He also asked for help from experts familiar with the Japanese armed forces. Dye assembled separate "American" and "Japanese" units, trained them in historically authentic combat tactics, and designed exercises during which the Japanese forces regularly encountered U.S. Marine forces in the jungle.

Central to the actors' training was an intense 12-day "boot camp" that took place in the rainforests near the cities of Port Douglas and Cairns in Far North Queensland. As soon as the primary cast arrived in Australia, Dye and his team picked them up and kicked off a daily training regimen that started at 0500 and sometimes lasted until 0200 on the following day. "We had to jam so much training into those 12 days that we had to really, really press hard," recalls Dye. "You wanted these folks to understand the spirit of *semper fidelis*. You really wanted them to have a little taste of that Marine Corps pride."

The full-immersion training cut the cast off from the outside world. They were treated like raw recruits from the start. "They lived in holes in the ground," explains Dye, "and usually ate twice a day." Dye's team simultaneously trained the Japanese contingent in a nearby area, and then began to "bump" the two units into each other so the actors could understand what meeting engagements in the jungle were like.

The physical requirements of the training were tough even for actor Jon Seda, who plays legendary Marine John Basilone in the miniseries. "I've boxed, wrestled and played football," says Seda, "but this was the most grueling and physically demanding thing I've ever been through. The boot camp taught us what we needed to know — how to walk, talk and look like a Marine. Once we were on set, we didn't have to act — we were *re*acting," says Seda. "We came out of boot camp and we were ready to go."

"Our purpose in training is so the actors can become the people that they're representing — mentally, spiritually and psychologically," explains Dye. "They didn't have to be taught how to take care of their weapons, how to take care of their gear, how to wear their uniforms. They knew how to do it right, and then they could focus on acting." Seda appreciated the rigorous nature of the boot camp. "There was no primping, no prima donna stuff," he says. "That was quickly thrown out on the first day." Seda recalls talking with a fellow actor on the third day of training, when the realism of the boot camp — the sweat, grime and exhaustion — was taking its toll on the cast. "I looked at him and said, 'What's going on? Are we actually training to go to war?' You completely forgot why you were there. That's how real they made it," Seda says.

## A proud legacy

While coordinating personnel and equipment for the production, McKenna found out something interesting: "Almost everybody who worked on this production had some sort of connection to the war," he recalls. "They had a grandfather who fought in the war, a grandmother who married an American, that kind of thing." In addition, local collectors supplied Japanese tanks and other authentic equipment from stocks that had remained in the area after the war ended.

What do members of the production staff hope that viewers will take away from watching *The Pacific*? "Marines are going to love this thing," says Dye. "It's dark, it's brutal — but so was the war in the Pacific. We didn't pull any punches." McKenna agrees: "It's by no means a puff piece," he says. "We're very honest. We show a lot of very brutal warfare that had to be done. You'll come away with a healthy respect for the tragedy of war, the necessity of winning that war, and the cost to the individual men to do so."

This applied to the cast as well. "I thought I knew a lot about World War II and enough about the military — about the sacrifices that were made," says Seda. Like the character he plays, Seda was born in New York, raised in New Jersey, and has a family of his own. "[The miniseries] changed my life as a husband and a father," says Seda. "This experience opened my eyes and my heart towards the sacrifices that were made and continue to be made for the freedom that is so often taken for granted."

Dye urges viewers to look at *The Pacific* from the perspective of today's wars in Iraq and Afghanistan. "When Marines see *The Pacific*, I want them to think, 'Look, that's my legacy. Those guys did this under the same kind of stress. I should do what the Corps demands of me, and I should do it gladly because these guys in the Pacific did it when it was their turn. What I'm seeing here is my legacy."

# QUIET WATERS, HEALING WARRIORS

*"Fishing is a solace ... the opposite of war ... a gentle and healing occupation."*
— *Luis Marden*

JOURNEY TO SOUTHWEST MONTANA between May and October and you'll see lots of people fishing, casting fly rods back and forth across the state's sparkling rivers. Fly fishing is an art unto itself, requiring a unique sense of style and a well-practiced level of skill. The men and women who spend their time along these Montana rivers do so out of love — a love of nature, of sport, of living a meaningful life.

Look a little closer and you'll realize that one of these river gatherings isn't a group of friends or family enjoying a fly-fishing trip. Instead, this group is comprised of wounded combat veterans from the wars in Iraq and Afghanistan. They've come together to learn about fly fishing, enjoy each other's company — and, most important, to relax and reflect on life after war.

This particular "mission" is different from anything these wounded warriors have experienced in the past. Their hosts are members of an organization called the Warriors & Quiet Waters Foundation. Using the medium of fly fishing, the Foundation provides therapeutic recreation and rehabilitation to traumatically injured servicemen and women.

Retired Marine Colonel Eric Hastings and a group of more than 300 volunteers lead these fishing expeditions, which last six to seven days each. During a typical year, the Foundation hosts five Fishing Experiences, or FX's, each with a group of six wounded warriors. An additional two FX's are sponsored specifically for married couples.

Participants come from all over the map: "We get our wounded warriors from hospitals on the West Coast, East Coast, and in between," explained Hastings, "and from Warrior Transition Units and Wounded Warrior Battalions integrated within operating forces and bases."

Hastings understands what these warriors have gone through: during his service in the Marine Corps he served as a pilot of F-8 fighters and A-4 attack aircraft in Viet Nam and deployed as Chief of Staff of Marine Forces/I-MEF for Operations Desert Shield and Storm. After he retired, Hastings and his wife Jean settled in the picturesque community of Bozeman, Montana.

**Building on a good idea**

Among their hobbies, the Hastings love to fish. In August 2006, while on a fly fishing trip to Canada, the couple discussed the day-to-day difficulties that wounded combat veterans experience — and possible ways to help those warriors adjust to life after the military.

Hastings had an idea. "Why don't we bring wounded warriors to Montana for some R&R?" he said to Jean. "We could use fly fishing as the focus."

The couple examined the concept, but they were reluctant to push ahead.

96

This was no part-time endeavor; running a program like this would require a full-time commitment.

"Like any good Marine," said Hastings, "I wrote a staff study to organize my thoughts, considering multiple ways of accomplishing a notional mission." Recalling the adage that "all servicemen bleed red," Hastings envisioned a program that supported any wounded warrior from the wars in Iraq or Afghanistan — regardless of his branch of service.

After finishing his staff study, Hastings planned his next move. In December of that year he and Jean flew from Bozeman to San Diego, Calif., to visit their two sons, who were serving on active duty. While he was there, Hastings decided to visit the Naval Regional Medical Center. He brought his close friend, Lieutenant Colonel Eric Jones, with him to the hospital.

"We met several severely wounded Marines, soldiers and sailors," recalled Hastings. "We spoke at length with Navy Captain Jennifer Town (Ret.), the hospital's new Comprehensive Combat Casualty Care Center executive." Town liked what she heard, and encouraged Hastings and Jones to continue developing their concept for a fly-fishing program.

**Putting the pieces together**

Not long after their trip the Hastings were reading a Bozeman newspaper when they came across an op-ed piece written by John Baden, a local economist and writer, about a conversation he had with Dr. Volney Steele, a retired local physician and medical historian.

Steele — by coincidence, a fly-fishing enthusiast — was concerned about post-combat treatment of wounded veterans. In the newspaper article, Steele proposed a concept that echoed Hastings' idea of providing R&R to wounded warriors via extended fishing trips. Baden challenged the public to take the concept seriously — and to do something about it.

In early January 2007, the Hastings invited Steele to their home to discuss the concept for their fishing program. "He came to our house and I said, 'Here's how we do it,' and I handed him my staff study," said Hastings.

"He read it ... and then we enthusiastically discussed ways of refining the mission and accomplishing an executable course of action."

Now it was time to do some outreach. Hastings and Steele advertised a series of public town-hall meetings. "Friends and fly fishing enthusiasts attended," recalled Hastings. "We discussed several alternatives, gaining enough consensus and voluntary help to proceed."

The result? The establishment of the Warriors & Quiet Waters Foundation, Inc., a 501(c)(3) nonprofit corporation staffed by a 10-member board of directors and funded by individual donations from several thousand individuals and businesses. Eventually the new organization signed up hundreds of volunteers to assist with everything from instructing to cooking to ground transportation.

In keeping with Hastings' original concept, from its inception the Foundation was a multi-service organization. Its 10-member board of directors has included members who served in the Marine Corps, Navy, Army and Air Force. Other directors have included a doctor, a dentist, business executives, entrepreneurs, an economist and writer, and a financial advisor.

To obtain equipment for the wounded warriors who would attend the fishing expeditions, the board of directors pitched their new program to vendors in the fishing industry. Support arrived from companies such as Rio Products (lines and accessories), Simms Fishing Products (fly fishing gear and clothing), Under Armor (clothing) and Suncloud Optics (high-performance sunglasses).

Local businesses in Bozeman got involved as well. Fly-fishing shops The Rivers Edge and Montana Troutfitters agreed to help. People offered their homes to provide lodging for the participants. Eventually the Foundation was able to lease a vacation home, the 356 Ranch, ensuring the wounded warriors a comfortable place to stay.

**First time out**

Eric Jones selected the first eight participants from the hospital ranks, and in

July 2007 — coinciding with an air show by the Blue Angels demonstration team — the Foundation hosted its first program in Bozeman. Another fishing expedition was held in late September of that year. For that FX the Foundation selected an additional six wounded warriors from the Naval Hospital in San Diego.

All of the participating veterans received a complete, all-expenses-paid package. "The program provides transportation, accommodations and meals," explained Hastings, "and gives each warrior a complete fly fishing outfit including rod, reel, line, leaders, flies, chest-pack, tools, boots, waders, shirt, cap and a bag to haul it all."

"Recently," added Hastings, "we also began giving [the warriors] a fly-tying kit and lessons in tying their own flies." At the end of the program, the warriors get to keep everything so they can continue fishing on their own.

## A growing effort

After a successful first year, the Foundation continued its efforts at a rapid pace. "Whether you are a beginner or a skilled angler, there are so many aspects of fishing that capture your interest," said Elyse End, a member of the Foundation's board of directors. "This includes the anticipation of what you will catch from below the surface of the water, as well as the focus and enjoyment of developing your skills. For the warriors, it becomes a 'can do' experience. They can use adaptive means to learn something new."

Army Sergeant First Class John Carter, a wounded warrior from Brooke Army Medical Center in San Antonio, Texas, was severely injured while he was deployed to Iraq. Carter lost his dominant arm and one of his legs. He was initially reluctant to participate in the fly-fishing program, but soon changed his mind.

"I had a great time," recalled Carter, "and even if I had not caught a single fish it would have still been tops. The scenery was great, the wildlife was awesome, and I could have just sat on the bank and imagined I was in heaven.

One day on Sixteen Mile Creek (one of the program's fishing locations) was like a year's worth of therapy."

The fishing experience is a two-way street: the participants and the staff learn a lot from each other. "One of the first warriors I worked with helped me to better understand Post Traumatic Stress Disorder and the current disruption in his life because of what he had experienced," said End.

The veteran told End about how the fishing experience — and the opportunity to spend time with other warriors — had a healing impact. "At the end of a day of fishing," End continued, "he said, 'Thank you so much. This was one of the best days of my life.'"

**Physical and mental benefits**

No matter how severe their physical challenges, all participants in the program learn to fly fish successfully. "We've had a wide variety of injuries and handicaps including single and double amputees, burn victims, and those with Traumatic Brain Injury and PTSD," explained Dave Kumlien, an entrepreneur and business owner who was instrumental in getting Warriors & Quiet Waters off the ground.

Kumlien noted that learning to fly fish helps with the veterans' existing rehabilitation programs. "They've actually discovered that the physical actions required to fly cast, handle the fly reel, and fly fish help them in their physical therapy," said Kumlien.

"I had one of my wounded warriors tell me that the three days he spent fly casting and fly fishing helped him regain more control and physical dexterity in his severely damaged arm and hand than he'd gained in the previous six months of physical therapy," said Kumlien. In fact, after completing his trip to Bozeman the veteran planned to continue fly fishing as part of his ongoing therapy.

The psychological benefits of the program are just as important as the physical benefits — perhaps more so.

"Our lives were forever and irreversibly changed by our experiences in combat," said Navy Corpsman Donryan Wiginton. "[And] I truly believe that our lives are now forever and irreversibly changed by our experiences in Bozeman, Montana. For the first time in four years I truly believe that I am going to be okay."

"I did more than learn how to fly fish," continued Wiginton. "I learned to let go. And that it was okay to let go and to live."

## A day on the water

What happens during a typical fishing expedition? Mornings begin with a home-cooked breakfast hosted by volunteer "moms." After that, "each day is a little different," said Tom O'Connor, secretary of the Foundation. A full day is devoted to training the participants in casting, followed by catching large trout from a stocked pond nearby. The warriors continue to develop their fly-fishing skills throughout the program.

"We pair each of the warriors (or couples) with a companion volunteer and an experienced guide for the three fishing days," said O'Connor. "We prefer that the volunteers be fly fishermen but we're not hard over on that. We ask that the companion volunteers not fish but rather be helpers and companions for the warriors."

Depending on the season, additional activities can include a trip to Yellowstone National Park, attending a football game at Montana State University, or participating in a concert — *Tchaikovsky's rousing 1812 Overture* — with the Bozeman Symphony Orchestra.

## A unique mix of participants

The Foundation focuses its efforts on three types of participant: those who are still on active duty, those who are near end-of-service, and those who have been medically or administratively discharged.

"We like to get them as soon as they've healed enough for such a program to be medically feasible," noted Hastings. "We had one double-amputee —

101

legs, above the knee — who participated in our program just two and a half months after his injury occurred."

Hastings added that many of the warriors have been hospitalized for six months to as long as two years, or have been transferred to administrative holding units. This results in a unique mix of participants.

Wounded warriors who lack full mobility learn how to take advantage of the physical capabilities that remain. One participant, Marine Corporal Matt Bradford, is blind and a double-leg amputee. None of that stopped him from taking a rod and reel and learning how to fly fish — with a little help from the guides and companion volunteers. For participants who travel by wheelchair only, Foundation staff members teach them how to fish from a seated position.

In some cases, specially modified equipment helps participants who have lost a hand or arm. The Foundation has rods with reels that can be operated with one hand. "Some of the wounded warriors learn to use their prosthetic hands and arms to take the fishing line off the reel," explained volunteer guide Mark Fogelsong, a member of the Foundation's board of directors. "Regardless of how the reel is operated, the basic casting stroke remains the same."

# SHORT STORIES

# WINGED EATERIES

IF YOU'VE EVER ENJOYED AN AIRLINE MEAL at 30,000 feet, how about a change of pace? Here are five restaurants where you can eat aboard an airplane without ever leaving the ground. By restoring and redecorating elderly aircraft, restaurant owners are creating new centerpieces for their establishments that serve as dining areas as well as colorful conversation pieces.

## El Avión Restaurant, Manuel Antonio, Costa Rica

The 1954-vintage C-123 cargo plane that forms the dining area of El Avión was originally used by the Nicaraguan Contras in the 1980s, then abandoned when the U.S. Iran-Contra Affair became public. With a fresh coat of paint and a shingled canopy protecting its metal fuselage, the plane now serves as a cliffside restaurant and bar for the Hotel Costa Verde, with a breathtaking view of the Pacific Ocean. The nearby national park hosts a variety of wildlife cavorting among white sand beaches and evergreen forests.

### Solo's Restaurant, Colorado Springs, Colorado, United States

Inside the fuselage of a retired Boeing KC-97 refueling aircraft is enough space to seat 42 customers. Pilot-turned-restaurateur Steve Kanatzar inserted the plane's left wing into an existing building to form a unique restaurant. The interior of the plane has been refitted with polished aluminum walls and comfortable booths, and the menu features moderately priced American dishes like burgers, chili, steaks, ribs and chicken.

### Runway 34 Restaurant, Zurich, Switzerland

In 2005 Swiss airline pilot Reto Seipel purchased a former Soviet Air Force Ilyushin Il-14 transport plane and had it flown to Zurich International Airport. The aircraft serves as a lounge for the new Runway 34 Restaurant, a glass-encased hangar near the airport's main runway. Chef Felix Berini, who received his training in top Swiss hotels and aboard the RMS *Queen Mary 2*, offers a variety of dishes from around the world.

### Jet Restaurant, Kleinhaugsdorf, Austria

A Russian Ilyushin Il-62 airliner abuts Excalibur City, a fantasy-themed shopping plaza perched on the Czech-Austrian border. Serving "the foods of five continents," the Jet Restaurant boasts colourful decorations by Austrian artist Ernst Fuchs and a menu that includes ostrich, New York steak and fried camembert with potatoes and cranberries. The dining area is accessible through two boarding bridges that extend from the shopping center, or from a set of air stairs rising from the parking lot.

### Western Grill Aircraft Restaurant, Dhaka, Bangladesh

In June 2006, Mustafa Aolad, a pilot and entrepreneur, rescued a crashed

Fokker F28 passenger plane and reinstalled it as an eatery in his hometown in Bangladesh. A two-story building underneath the left wing houses the kitchen, washrooms and a waiting area. Patrons enjoy drinks in the waiting area, then climb a spiral staircase into the plane to enjoy Chef Sushanto Kosta's 55-item buffet of Bangladeshi, Chinese, Continental and Thai cuisine. You can dine in the main cabin or, for a small additional charge, in business class.

# WIDE LOAD:
# ELEPHANT TRANSPORT

THE AIR FORCE'S MAMMOTH C-17 GLOBEMASTER III cargo plane transports everything from troops to supplies to ammunition. In November 2006 it carried a payload of an entirely different type: an African elephant named Maggie.

A resident of the Alaska Zoo for nearly a quarter century and the only elephant in the state, Maggie was having increasing difficulty in her often-chilly concrete environment. A grassroots campaign convinced zoo officials to allow Maggie to move to a warmer, more comfortable home: the 2,300-acre ARK 2000 wildlife sanctuary in northern California operated by the Performing Animal Welfare Society, or PAWS.

All that PAWS needed was a safe method of transporting Maggie from Alaska to California. No commercial airliners were big enough to hold her, so PAWS sought help from the U.S. Air Force. Gen. Michael Moseley, the Air Force chief of staff, approved a mission to carry Maggie aboard a C-17 at a cost to PAWS of $200,000. The Air Force labeled the mission "Operation Maggie Migration."

Since the Air Force couldn't simply walk Maggie into the C-17's cargo bay, she was provided with a gigantic reinforced metal crate weighing 10,000 pounds and measuring 10 by 8 by 18 feet. Locked safely inside the crate, she was then driven from the zoo to Elmendorf Air Force Base near Anchorage, Alaska. There, Air Force personnel moved Maggie on a conveyor belt through the C-17's rear clamshell doors and into the airplane's massive cargo bay.

At 8,000 pounds, Maggie weighed just a fraction of the C-17's maximum payload of 170,900 pounds. For the most part the aircraft handled the same as with most types of cargo, except when its wheels were on the ground: "If Maggie rocked back and forth in her crate," recalls Capt. Blake Johnson, who led the mission, "you could feel it, similar to the rocking of a car."

In planning the mission, Johnson consulted with Maggie's veterinarian to determine the best settings for cabin pressure and deck angle during takeoff and descent. "We treated her like a distinguished visitor," says Johnson. "We minimized acceleration and deceleration, and flew at a maximum altitude of 25,000 feet to keep the cabin altitude (pressurization) to a minimum." The temperature in the cargo bay was set at around 70 degrees.

After a five-hour flight the C-17 touched down at Travis Air Force Base in northern California. Maggie's crate was placed on a flatbed truck for the 85-mile drive to the sanctuary near San Andreas.

Johnson appreciated the experience of having an elephant as a passenger in his C-17. "It's not something we do every day," he laughs.

# LOST AND FOUND AT LAX

HAVE YOU EVER BEEN LATE FOR A FLIGHT, then rifled through your pockets only to realize that you've lost your cell phone, wallet or jewelry on your way through the airport terminal? Each year 70 million harried people pass through security checkpoints at Los Angeles International Airport — and often leave something behind. In one month, travelers forgot nearly 500 personal items at Terminal 1 alone. Multiply that average number across the nine terminals at LAX and you have a huge stockpile of odds and ends that rival any museum collection: watches, keys, toys, loose change, even dentures and baby seats. "You name it, we find it," says Nico Melendez, public affairs manager for the Transportation Security Administration's Pacific region, which supervises the airport security checkpoints.

111

So where do all of these orphaned items go? They're placed in heavy plastic bins and delivered once a day to the TSA Lost and Found office just down the street from the airport. In a dim, overstuffed storeroom that resembles an unfinished basement, a staff of 15 TSA officers inspects, logs, and stores each item until the owner is found — or 30 days go by, whichever comes first. "After a month," says Melendez, "if we can't locate the owner, items valued at less than $500 are destroyed or donated to a non-profit agency," while high-value items are sent to the General Services Administration, a government organization that manages federal property.

Inside the Lost and Found office, shelves 15 feet deep groan under rows of 12-gallon plastic bins, each stuffed with enough clothing to outfit entire families. A forgotten walker leans against one shelving unit, near several lonely umbrellas wondering where their owners went. Alfred Howard, the logistics manager for the Lost and Found office, pulls open the doors to a six-foot-tall safe. Inside are Howard's most expensive customers: high-tech gear like laptop computers, flash drives, luxury watches and cell phones. "We collect over 400 cell phones each week," he says. If the owners aren't found within the 30-day limit, the cell carriers instruct TSA to destroy the phones. Driver's licenses are also destroyed if not claimed. Lost passports, however, travel to the State Department in Washington, D.C., for disposition.

If your bank account is suddenly a little light, perhaps you unwittingly donated some money to the government on your way through the airport. Thousands of dollars in bills and coins flow through the Lost and Found every week. "Recently we found $5,000 in a bowl at one of our security checkpoints," recalls Howard. No one called to claim the money, so it was sent to the U.S. Treasury, where it was placed in the general fund. That's the account where your income tax payments reside. "Someone paid his taxes twice," muses Howard.

The most popular item at the Lost and Found? Hold onto your pants: each week, up to 500 travelers at LAX forget their belts. Although metal buckles aren't likely to trigger the x-ray alarm system, many people take their belts off anyway — and abandon them as they rush to catch a flight. While this might be understandable, it gets weirder: some people forget their shoes at the security checkpoints. "You'd think that if someone left their shoes behind, they'd come back to get them," chuckles Melendez.

Each month nearly 650 people phone the LAX Lost and Found office to claim a personal item.

# RESTORING
# A RESTAURANT B-17

FOR THREE DECADES, HUNGRY PATRONS of the State Armory Bar in Greeley, Colo., ate underneath a B-17 fuselage that hung from the ceiling of the theme restaurant. According to rumor the aircraft had been used as a soundstage mock-up for the 1949 film *Twelve O'Clock High* as well as the TV series of the same name. In 2007 the California Air Heritage Foundation rescued the fuselage for restoration and brought it to Los Angeles, where the B-17 had originally rolled off the Douglas Aircraft assembly line during World War II.

How did a B-17 end up adorning the interior of a restaurant? When the Twentieth Century Fox studio sold off many of its props during the 1970s, a restaurant owner obtained the fuselage and shipped it to Colorado.

Over the next 30 years Foundation director Bruce Orriss repeatedly tried to purchase the B-17, to no avail. When the restaurant owner sold his interest in the business, he finally agreed to cut the airplane loose. Clark Enterprises Construction Company of Eaton, Colo., opened up one of the restaurant's walls to remove the bomber, and Blossom, Texas-based Chapman Trucking drove the B-17 to California.

# ABOUT THE AUTHOR

ALLAN T. DUFFIN is a writer/producer. A veteran of the U.S. Air Force, he is the co-author, with Darryl Kimball, of *Takedown: How an Undercover Cop Dismantled the Biggest Drug-Smuggling Ring in Maine* and *Catch the Sky: The Adventures and Misadventures of a Police Helicopter Pilot*; author of *History in Blue: 160 Years of Women Police, Sheriffs, Detectives, and State Troopers*; and co-author of *The "12 O'Clock High" Logbook: The Unofficial History of the Novel, Motion Picture, and TV Series*. His Web site is www.aduffin.com.

www.ingramcontent.com/pod-product-compliance
Lightning Source LLC
Chambersburg PA
CBHW071005040426
42443CB00007B/668